Coping WITH TEACHERS

PETER COREY

Illustrated by Martin Brown

Scholastic Children's Books
Scholastic Publications Ltd,
7–9 Pratt Street, London NW1 0AE, UK

Scholastic Inc.,
730 Broadway, New York, NY 10003, USA

Scholastic Canada Ltd,
123 Newkirk Road, Richmond Hill,
Ontario, Canada L4C 3G5

Ashton Scholastic Pty. Ltd,
P O Box 579, Gosford, New South Wales,
Australia

Ashton Scholastic Ltd,
Private Bag 1, Penrose, Auckland,
New Zealand

Published by Scholastic Publications Ltd, 1991
Text copyright © Peter Corey, 1991
Illustrations copyright © Martin Brown, 1991

ISBN 0 590 76485 3

Printed by Cox & Wyman, Reading, Berks.
Typeset in Plantin by AKM Associates (UK) Ltd., Southall, London

Contents...

Dedication...

I wasn't very good at school. But then, I blame the teachers. Well, why not? After all, everybody else does, don't they? Think about it. If a child starts smoking, swearing or going out with goats, its parents say: "Must have picked it up at school" (the bad habit, I mean, not the goat). But if the same child comes home with 48 GCSEs and a cup for swimming, the same parents say: "Takes after me!". The poor old teacher doesn't get a mention. So, since teachers have to put up with lack of respect, lack of chalk and lack of money, I'd like to dedicate this book to them. Most sincerely. And, having done so, I can now get down to being really rude about them!

Peter Corey

Preface .....

"Those who can, do. Those who can't, teach." I wonder who said that? Not Shakespeare, I know that much. He only wrote in iambic pentameter and, as you know, the square on the pentameter is equal to some of the squares on the hippopotamus, or something. Anyway, if it hadn't got identical twins or girls dressed up as blokes in it, Shakespeare wasn't interested.

But who did say it? If I'd paid attention at school, I'd know. But I didn't. In fact I didn't pay anything at school. Except dinner money, and that not very often. I mean, I don't see why I should subsidise State-approved mass poisoners, do you? Oh! I forgot! I did once, at secondary school, pay protection money to another boy. Until I realised that he was smaller than me. Much smaller. In fact he was a first year from the nearby infant school, who had just popped round with a note for the games teacher, and took the opportunity to exercise a little enterprise initiative. He married her, actually. It was a quiet affair. Just the school (all 1047 of us). The honeymoon was a bit of a rushed job, as she was on playground duty and he was on detention. But not all pupils have such a close relationship with their teachers, it may surprise you to learn. It's probably just as well!

This book will endeavour to identify the problem of teachers, and suggest a way of coping with it. Naturally it will not attempt to solve the problem. This is of course impossible, since teachers are "grown-ups" (even if they don't behave like it) and, as you will already know, solving any problem that involves dealing with grown-ups is a complete waste of time. However, after reading this book, perhaps you will feel better equipped to cope. I do hope so!

Teachers—
the Root of the Problem

Writing a book about teachers is not easy. For one thing, what if they catch me? Will I be made to stand in the corner? Kept in? Who knows! You can never tell with teachers. The minute you find you've done something worthy of a good telling-off, they praise you for your ingenuity. But if you use your head, they bite it off. You can't win. But then, no-one ever said that life had to be fair. No. Life's a pig, and then you die. But in the meantime . . . you gotta go to school!

Someone once said: "Schooldays are the happiest days of your life." It was obviously someone who played a lot of truant! How can they be the happiest days of your life? After all, which would you rather be doing:

(*a*) sitting in a boiling hot classroom, trying to learn something that you know is never going to be of any use to you;
or
(*b*) playing or lazing around in the sunshine?

If you answered (a) you're probably an idiot. Or a teacher (it can be the same thing). After all, teachers *choose* to stand around in classrooms, don't they? It's part of the job. It might even be the best part for some of them, who knows? After all, they're not normal, are they? They can't be. No-one in their right mind would enjoy spending their entire life in school. But that's what they do, isn't it? They go to school as children, then college and university, and then back to school. Weird or what? No wonder they're a problem. But let's start right at the beginning . . .

What is a Teacher?

As always, the best place to start when trying to answer a question as complex as "What is a teacher?" is a dictionary. Well, usually, anyway. But not in this case. In this case my Pick-Pocket edition of the *Concise Oxford* can only offer me:

Teacher: *n*. Person who teaches, esp. in a school.

Brilliant! Mind you, when I tell you that the same book tells me that a "teacup" is (and I quote): "a cup for drinking tea", you'll probably realise what I'm up against. I wonder who writes such uninformative drivel? Teachers, probably. So, in the absence of any form of expert help, let's resolve the question scientifically.

Imagine that you are in a classroom. (That can't be too difficult. It's somewhere you visit an average of five times a week, unless you're particularly expert at forging sick notes.) So, you're in a classroom. That person at the front doing all the talking is the teacher. (By the way, that person at the *back* doing all the talking is next in line for detention.) But, yes indeed, that chatterbox standing out at the front who seems to know all the answers is the teacher. I say *seems*, because they probably don't know all the answers. The best way to find out is to ask them a question. It usually sorts out the wheat from the chaff.

Now that you know which one is the teacher, the best thing to do is to keep your eye on them. This will give the teacher the impression that you are listening, which is always worth a million Brownie points because it's the sort of stuff teachers are really keen on. Being listened to. And you can see why. After all, what's the point of going to university to gain all that knowledge, and then teacher

training camp to learn how to pass it on, if nobody is going to listen to you, eh? Of course, you don't actually have to listen, just give the impression that you are. That should work fine. Unless they ask you a question. But if you're really clever you'll have perfected the art of answering a question with another question. No, that's not right. If you're really clever you'll know the answer. But if you're really *cunning* (that's more like it!) you'll answer the question with another question. For instance:

Teacher: What is the capital of Indonesia?
You: Which Indonesia?

No. Sorry. That's a bad example. Anyway, you get the rough idea. Maybe it'll just be easier to listen.

So the one at the front doing the talking is probably the teacher. (If they're about a hundred and two with a bald head, that's usually a clincher.) What can you do about it? Not a lot, I'm afraid. They do say that "an apple a day keeps the doctor away". I suppose that you could experiment to find out what has the same effect on teachers. But that's only a temporary solution, and you really need something more permanent. Particularly if you're fool enough to go to university. Sorry, I'll rephrase that. I mean particularly if you're bright enough to be fool enough to want to go to university. Or something. The whole point is that, in order to ensure that you are immune from the problem of teachers, you need to know what makes them tick. And, when they stop ticking, how long you've got to run for cover before they explode. There's nothing more lethal than teacher-fallout. I know. I've fallen out with a few of them in my time. But let's try and answer the next question.

Where do teachers come from?

Think about the other pupils in your class. Go on — force yourself. I know it can be unpleasant in some cases, but it's all in the interests of science. Think specifically about their ambitions. What they want to be when they leave school. Or what they want to be when they grow up, whichever happens first. The kid with specs who sits near the window ... what was it he said he wanted to be? An astrophysicist, wasn't it? And the big kid with spots ... the twenty-three-stone one who has to sit near the door and be shoe-horned into his desk ... he wants to be an internationally famous sex-symbol, doesn't he? Then there's the kid with bits of dead animal in his pocket ... vet, was it? Or something in cosmetics? But think hard if any of them ever told you that they wanted to be a teacher (when they were in their right mind, I mean, not just after they'd been hanging from the wallbars for six hours or eaten a double helping of Spotted Dick, cooked as only the school dinner ladies know how.)

Can you recall a single person, in their right mind and not under any duress or being tortured by the Ninja Monitors, tell you to your face that they wanted to be a teacher? Can you, eh? Put your hand on your heart and say that you can. Go on! (Your heart's on the left, by the way. I learned that at school . . . or was it at the pictures?) Anyway, you can't, can you? You cannot honestly say that anyone has ever told you that they wanted to become a teacher, can you? Well, neither can I. In all the years I was at school I never heard anyone say they wanted to be a teacher. Not even any of the teachers ever said they wanted to be a teacher. And we pupils used to ask each other a lot in those days. After all, there were lots of jobs to choose from then. You could take your pick — especially if you wanted to be a navvy (ha! ha!). But no-one ever told me that they wanted to be a teacher. Oh, hang on. I tell a lie. Stan Jinks said he wanted to be a teacher. Oh, no! He didn't! He said *tea-chest*. He wanted to be a tea-chest:

Tea-Chest: Large wooden chest for storing tea. (*Concise Oxford* again!)

We laughed at poor Stan, as you can probably imagine. Boy, did we give him some stick! But the laugh was on us in the end, because he made it. He became a tea-chest. Not much of a life, I don't reckon, but at least he got the chance to travel and see the world, even if it was from the holds of cargo ships. But still, no-one comes to mind who ever expressed even the slightest desire to be a teacher. *Set fire to* a teacher — yes. *Be* a teacher — no. Except my brother, but he doesn't count. But then he doesn't need to count because he teaches geography. So where do all these teachers come from? Assuming that teachers are in fact just grown-up versions of ordinary school children, how do they come into being? What makes a perfectly sane five-year-old would-be fire engine driver suddenly change course in mid-career and take up teaching? Has it got anything to do with the examination structure in this country? Let us investigate that possibility.

Pass the exams Please..

The way the system works is that basically the more exams you pass, the better the choice of jobs available to you. In theory at least. It's rather like a fair-ground stall, where the little pyramids of tin cans represent exam passes and the beanbags you throw at them represent your chance to gain those passes. The fluffy toys, diseased goldfish and sachets of toxic bubblebath represent job opportunities. Oh, and the scruffy-looking bloke standing there taking the money and scratching his backside represents your teacher. Hmm. Quite a resemblance. Anyway, you get the picture. So: the more tin-cans (exam passes) you knock off the shelf with the beanbags, the better the prize. As Bruce Forsyth would probably say, given half a chance: "Passes mean Prizes". Here's a rough guide to just what your winnings could mean to you in today's job market:

Number of passes	Job opportunities
Ten or more	lawyer/ barrister/ teacher/ astrophysicist/neurosurgeon
Eight to ten	captain of industry
Six to eight	scientist/ doctor
Four to six	vet/ TV presenter
Two to four	politician/ best-selling author/ farmer/ newspaper magnate/ dustman/ nurse/
One to two	supermarket checkout operative/ airline steward/ train driver/ fireman/ postman/ ballet dancer

None ....millionaire/ high court judge/ pope/ filmstar/ prime minister/ queen/ king/ duke/ earl/ lord/ disco dancer/ female impersonator*/ etc. etc.

(* I don't think a female impersonator needs much of an education, unless of course they want to marry into the Royal Family. Which is odd, because you don't need to be bright to be Royal.)

As you can see, you need to be pretty bright to be a teacher, whereas the traditionally popular jobs require less of an education. So one can only assume that your average teacher is in fact a weak-willed would-be train driver, postman or nurse who gets badgered into becoming a teacher by the school Careers Officer. And what is a Careers Officer? Another teacher! Another over-qualified would-be postman or ballet dancer! But what makes them do it? Why do people become teachers in the first place? To understand this, we need to examine the history of education.

Who invented School?

No-one really knows. I mean, teaching has gone on since the beginning of time. Without it we would not know how to do anything. When you're born, there are only a limited number of functions you can perform instinctively. And most of those are bodily functions. If you catch my drift! So someone has to teach you how to cope. This leads to being taught how to speak, read, fight your brother, etc. In fact, much of life is a learning experience: pouring scalding hot tea into your ear teaches you where your mouth is — you hear it going "Aaar!!!!!"; crossing the road and ending up under a bus teaches you road safety; and getting arrested by the police teaches you to be a bit more devious in future!

All this teaching leads quite naturally towards organised education, in a school. But who actually had the idea? I think it just evolved, basically. The ancient civilisations, like Greece, had philosophers who taught small groups of young men, through discussion. The groups probably steadily grew, it started to rain, they all went indoors, and so schools were born. I expect thats roughly how it happened. I don't know who introduced all the other school things like dinners and so forth. I expect that was someone who was secretly trying to close the schools down. But let's examine the educational developments more closely.

ANCIENT GREECE

The average Greek schoolday consisted of a bit of learning, a lot of sport and a fair amount of fighting. It's amazing how little schools have changed, really, isn't it? Mind you, when the Ancient Greeks were philosophising and wrestling each other with nothing on, we Britons were running about covered in blue paint, going "Ug!". Nowadays that's more or less reversed. We've got double glazing, Sir Jimmy Saville and the Reliant Robin, and what have the Greeks got? The Doner Kebab. Which only goes to prove that education can be a dangerous thing, if proof were needed.

You may have noticed that I said that Ancient Greek philosophers taught "groups of young men", and not "groups of young people". This is because the Ancient Greeks, and indeed all of the civilisations of the ancient world, didn't believe that it was necessary to educate a woman. As long as she could peel an egg, boil a yam, stuff a goat or kebab an aardvark, it didn't really matter that she couldn't hold her own in an after-dinner conversation about the latest writings of Plato. (Though why anyone should want to waste their time talking about Mickey Mouse's dog beats me.)

Anyway, pretty soon some of the women were revolting

(well, it was very hot and there wasn't much soap about). They were insisting on equality. They were tired of being tied to the kitchen sink — it made it very difficult to get down to the shops. They started saying: "We ain't not putting up with it no more." (They hadn't had an education, so they didn't know how to speak properly, remember!) One of them, Lysistrata, even suggested that they should witthold their husbands' "marital rights" — clean socks, ironed underpants and warmed slippers, etc. — until they had got equality. That did the trick. However, with equality came full-time (compulsory) education for girls. You might have known there'd be a catch!

The armies of Ancient Rome spread the concept of education as far afield as Britain, where the Angles, Jutes,

Picts, Scots and Gauls lived a miserable existence in mud huts, with nothing more exciting to look forward to than the weekly stoat-baiting or an occasional Cliff Richard concert. So, naturally, the idea of going to school was quite appealing. And when they were told that the alternative was being disembowelled with a blunt olive branch, they readily acquiesced. (Oh, come on! You go to school! You know what it means! OK, OK! I'll admit I had to look it up, if it makes you feel better!) Ah! The Ancient Romans! Another great civilisation with a strong belief in organised education. And where are they now? They can't even win the World Cup! More proof of the folly of education, I'd say!

HENRY TUDOR CHICKEN LEG

Tudor England: a time when Britain was well on the way to being able to boast that *Britannia Rules the Waves*, even if they hadn't commissioned the song yet. OK, so the *Mary Rose* sank before it even got as far as the Isle of Wight, but then they didn't have GCSE Woodwork in those days.

Some years later, Sir Walter Raleigh singed the King of Spain's beard, using a very long match. He then invented the bicycle. An educated man, obviously. And, of course, most of the educated people in Elizabethan England were men, because they still weren't sold on the idea of educated women, even though they had a queen on the throne. Mind you, that was more by accident than design. Henry VIII, Elizabeth's father, had been trying for a boy and had got through six wives in the process. He kept chopping their heads off which, even with the scantest of sex education, you will realise is not how babies are made. But they didn't really know much about babies in those days. They'd never

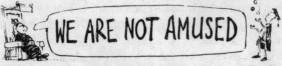

even heard of Doctor Spock (or Kirk and Scottie).

It wasn't really until Henry gave up being king and retired to a little country castle called *Dunrulin*, that he started improving himself. He even started writing songs. *Greensleeves* was his big hit. It got to number one — mainly because anyone who refused to buy a copy had their fingernails removed. He knew a thing or two about marketing, did Henry, even if he wasn't very bright! But that wasn't really Henry's fault. After all, in the 16th century a monarch's education consisted of the three "R"s: Ruling, Ruling and Ruling. You were better off being a playwright, like Shakespeare.

The Bard of the Avon Ladies

Shakespeare was an educated man. He knew Greek and Latin. Mind you, he wasn't so hot on English or spelling, at least not if his plays are anything to go by. Shakespeare was a teacher. Did you know that? Probably explains why his plays are so difficult to follow.

WE ARE NOT AMUSED

Victorian England: I realise that this is a bit of a jump from the 16th century, but Victorian schools have more bearing on the school of today. Let's face it, many of our schools are still Victorian. Even some of the teachers are the same ones they had then. So, what were the schools like? Very strict, in a word. (Sorry, in two words. I was away when they did counting at school.) "Spare the rod and spoil the child." This was one of the maxims of Victorian school life. What did it mean? I don't know, but logic tells me that it has something to do with fishing. All I know is that Victorian school life made your average schoolchild quake in their boots — those who could afford them. The rest just had to make do with quaking in their bare feet, which is not nearly as easy.

The teacher ruled the classroom with a rod of iron, except in Sheffield, where they used stainless steel with a hallmark. They only taught three things — the three "R"s, which now stood for Reading, Riting and Rithmetic (they still weren't that hot on spelling). Of course, rich people's children went to public schools, so named because the general public weren't allowed to go there. At the public schools, in addition to the three "R"s pupils had cold showers, fagging, flogging, bullying and roasting bare buttocks in front of a log fire. But then, after all, they were the *privileged classes*. The rest of us had to go without these things.

The education of women was still not considered a priority. Not until Emily Pankhurst chained herself to some railings outside the Houses of Parliament, thus

preventing the MPs from parking their bikes. As a result of this, women were given the vote and MPs were given a pay-rise so that they could all buy cars.

Strangely enough, even though their education was frowned upon, many women became teachers. Was this a way of getting their own back? Well, it could have been, although it's far more likely that teaching was one of the few acceptable professions for a woman to enter. You see, the idea of women working was not acceptable to many men (mainly because it did them out of a job, I suspect!). So the only job opportunities open to women were things like nanny, governess, shop assistant and teacher. But not a lot else. There were no female pop stars, for instance. If there had been, Des O'Connor would never have done as well as he did, even though he's got lovely legs.

Oh what a lovely war

However, it was the Victorian era that introduced the concept (on any sort of large scale) of the schoolmistress. Up until then a mistress was something Lord Nelson had, and Lady Nelson turned a blind eye to. Bit of a coincidence them both having a blind eye, isn't it?

The early half of the twentieth century was significant for its wars. Naturally there had been wars before, but this was the first time that everyone was allowed to join in. There were two main ones. First, the First World War, known also as the "Great War". And second, the Second World War, known also as the "Pretty Good But Not As Good As The Last One War". The school system, the teaching of the three "R"s, survived the two World Wars more or less intact, although some of the public schools did add "killing" to the curriculum, just in case the wars went into extra time. Obviously there have been other wars

since, but none that have had such a marked effect on
education. It was realised that, if the peoples of Europe
were going to spend much of the twentieth century
fighting each other, it made sense to be able to speak each
other's languages. After all, there's not a lot of point yelling
insults at your enemy if he has no idea what you're
shouting about, is there? French had already been added to
the curriculum some time earlier, and had proved its worth
in both World Wars, as they were largely fought in France
(because they'd got the best battlefields). For instance, it
made ordering a meal in a French restaurant after a hard
day's fighting much easier. Not that you could get much
more than frogs and snails, because of food rationing, but
still.

In the fifties the school curriculum was expanded to include other modern languages. Many schools stopped teaching Latin, realising that we were no longer under threat of attack from Julius Caesar.

The sixties was the period of Flower-power, the Beatles and the Mini-skirt. All of which had it's effect on education. "Make Love — Not War" was the cry. This meant that Killing had to be taken off the syllabus, and restricted to the games field or the playground, and Sex Education had to be taught instead. Which was not as easy as might at first be thought, mainly because schools couldn't get the textbooks then. So, until someone could quickly write and publish one (preferably with pictures), pupils had to rely on their teacher's knowledge of the subject. Which explains a lot! After all, many teachers didn't seem to know too much about the subject they'd spent three years at university studying. How could they possibly be expected to understand something as complex as Sex?

THE SEVERE SEVENTIES

When the history books are written, two things will stand out from the seventies: Graffitti and Margaret Thatcher as Education Minister. And, strangely, one of the earliest uses of Graffitti was to proclaim "Maggie Thatcher Milk

Snatcher!" on school walls everywhere. This was because Mrs Thatcher did away with free school milk, in an effort to get more people to go to the dentist due to a lack of calcium. There has always been a great debate about Graffitti, as people cannot make their minds up whether it's just ugly and unpleasant, or very clever. The same was also true of Mrs Thatcher!

The 'Ateful Eighties.

Graffitti and Thatcherism were still with us in the eighties. Graffitti had almost achieved respectability. Naturally it had a profound effect on education, in particular on spelling. The media didn't help. They started using phonetic spelling in adverts etc., instead of the "proper" spellings. Mind you, this just served to draw attention to the stupidities of the English language. After all, if S.O.X. doesn't spell SOCKS, what does it spell?

The Eighties were also significant for the introduction of "Baker Days", which we still have to this day. These are days when all the pupils are given time off, so that teachers can go into school and take it in turns teaching each other. They sit in your desk. They probably use your text books. They may *even* take a nibble at the chewing gum you left stuck to the lid! Blooming cheek, I say!

The Baker Day system can be a real eye opener for some young teachers, who up until then have not had teaching experience, even though they have been working in schools for some time! "Baker Days" were named after their inventor, Kenneth Baker, not to be confused with Hilda Baker, a popular comedienne from the 50's/60's. Kenneth was taller, for one thing. Also they used to say of Hilda: "She knows, you know". No-one ever said that about

25

Kenneth! Kenneth it was who thought that 6 plus 6 = 13. This became known as the Baker's Dozen!

Throughout the Sixties, Seventies and Eighties, the school curriculum kept expanding, thus introducing a broader range of teachers into our lives.

 So now you know how teachers got there, but we're still no nearer to finding out the answer to that crucial question . . .

What makes them tick?

My biggest problem in attempting to answer this question was just where to start. What I wanted was a hand-picked team of experts, all of whom would have something to *give*. (Unlike my book *Coping With Parents*, where the team of experts all appeared to have something to *take*. By the time the book was finished, my home looked like a swarm of locusts had swept through it. I've never fully refurnished it. We're still eating off orange boxes.) So, I wasn't going to get caught out like that again. Oh no. But where would I find good, reliable, honest experts? Well, I tried good old *Yellow Pages*. After letting my fingers do the walking for several days, I was no nearer to my goal. (I had, however, managed to locate a first edition of *Fly Fishing* by J.R. Hartley, so it wasn't a complete waste of time.)

The real problem was that I didn't really know what I was looking for. What sort of person would be an expert on teachers? Not a teacher, certainly! I suppose that's reasonable, really. I mean, one doesn't expect a plumber to know anything about plumbing. Well, one does but they don't. So why should a teacher know anything about teachers? So, in the absence of any real expert to call on, I decided to tackle the task single-handed. By which I mean on my own, rather than with one arm tied behind my back!

I get stuck in

First of all I needed to discover just what sort of people teachers are. Get behind that cloud of chalk-dust and academic bluster, and discover the person beneath the Marks and Spencer's cardigan. I felt that it could be a bit like ripping the *Phantom of The Opera*'s mask off. I would never know what horrors lay beneath, but I had to do it.

I started hanging around outside schools in order to try and catch teachers in unguarded moments. All this brought me for my pains was wet socks and a warning from the police. So a change of tactic was called for. I decided to try and observe teachers in their free time. I joined badminton clubs and rambling societies. I started collecting stamps and drinking Real Ale. I even joined a local amateur dramatics society, having been reliably informed that half the membership were teachers. That got me

nothing but a small part in a musical written by the head of liberal studies at a large comprehensive, about the history of motorised transport. I played the back end of a bus. It was terrible. I think I'd rather have worked for Andrew Lloyd Webber. At least he writes songs you can whistle. Occasionally. But it was while I was in this production, in fact during the middle of the Saturday evening performance (we only did it three times, thank the Lord!), that I got my first breakthrough. My costume split. And during the sewing-up operation, performed by a teacher of home economics (a very nice man), I learned that the thing to do was to join MENSA. You've heard of MENSA, I imagine. It's what the popular press call *The Club For Brainy Folk*. Anyway, apparently a very large number of teachers belong to it. Yes, I can tell you're as amazed as I was, and I was dumbfounded. Teachers — intelligent? This was a revelation. So, they were only pretending to be stupid. Why? I mentally added this to the list of questions I would eventually need to get answered, and sent off my application form.

Joining MENSA was considerably easier than I had imagined. Naturally there was an entrance test, and they checked that I could pay the entrance fee (which I put down on expenses — publisher please note!). But the entrance test was a walk-over, not to say a surprise. In fact, it was more like an audition. I had to sing a song, for which I had to provide my own sheet music, and do a speech from Shakespeare. I chose the baby-eating scene from *Coriolanus*, which in retrospect I think might have been a mistake, as they were interviewing me over a working lunch. Still, we managed to keep their lunch down, and I was in. A member of MENSA, no less! And they hardly asked me any questions. Oh, apart from was I allergic to nylon tights, and did I have my own make-up box? I should have smelt a rat, I suppose, but I didn't, so blinded was I by my quest to discover what made teachers tick.

It wasn't until MENSA sent me to a war zone to play a bilious comedy colonel in a farce called *Ooops! There Goes The Elastic!*, that I discovered I hadn't joined MENSA at all! I'd joined ENSA, the war-time entertainments squad. I hadn't realised it still existed, but apparently this branch was kept going by a bunch of old soldiers who just love dressing up. But, the question is: whose fault was it that I'd joined ENSA and not MENSA? Was it a genuine mistake on the part of the teacher who had directed me there in the first place? Or was it part of a sinister and devious plot to prevent me getting to the truth about teachers? This begged another question: were teachers incredibly devious and clever? Or were they stupid? I added these questions to my mental list, and returned my kidney donor card to ENSA headquarters, along with the seamless tights. ("Kidney donor card?" I hear you ask. "What is he on about?" Well, apparently they issue organ donor cards in certain branches of the services, in case you get stuck in the desert and food supplies run low. I thought you'd like to know that. You see, this book is informative, just as you would expect a book about teachers to be.) Ah, yes! That's what this book is about: Coping *With Teachers*! I realised that I was no nearer to solving the problem. A change of tactics was called for. See Appendix 5.

Teachers I have known

A trip to the attic secured my old diaries. I always amazed myself when I was at school that I even bothered to keep a diary. I didn't bother to do much else. But I must say that it's proved invaluable as a social history. Not to mention being very handy as an *aide-memoire* (that's foreign!) on the odd occasions that I bump into old school chums. Except of course these are always odd occasions, and I never have my diary with me. Why is it that you only ever bump into old school mates when you're somewhere strange? Like at a meeting of an obscure religious sect, or halfway up a mountain? Or at Butlins? What law of probability governs this fact? The same law that governs the fact that you only ever bump into one of your old teachers if you're doing something naughty, like robbing a bank . . . .?

"Right, give me the money and be quick about it! Oh! Hello, sir!"

"Johnson isn't it? See me afterwards, boy!"

"Yes, sir!"

It's the same law that governs the fact that every time you're involved in a road accident that leaves you totally unharmed but results in the complete removal of your trousers, you see that girl from the fifth year that you really fancy. Well, that's my experience anyway. Happens every time.

Of course, without a diary, chance encounters with old school mates can be embarrassing, because the memory can play tricks. The one and only time I bumped into an old school mate was on a crash course for a charity parachute jump. I had gone along to jeer. He hadn't changed a bit. He hadn't even got taller, and I hadn't seen him since Infants. Mind you, I later discovered that he had made 342 charity parachute jumps, so that could explain his height. The conversation went something like:

"Eggy!" (We called him *eggy* because of an odour problem he had.) "Eggy! How are you? Cor! I haven't seen you since we got that first year's head stuck down the toilet! Cor! Did we laugh! We thought he was going to die!"

"Yes. And we were right!"

How embarrassing! I really should have remembered it. They say that your school days are the best years of your life, but what's the point if you forget all the best bits?

But it's the teachers we're interested in, isn't it? I scanned my diaries for little tell-tale signs that would help prove or disprove the theories I was forming in my mind about teachers. Here are some random thoughts that I gleaned from the diaries:

Mr Pargetter: Metalwork teacher. We called him Percy. Mainly because his initial was 'P'. But it could just as easily have stood for Paul or Peregrine, or a real teacher's name — like Prudence. Let's face it, we really knew nothing about him. He certainly didn't look like a teacher. Not even a metalwork one. Although, since he was the only metalwork teacher I'd ever seen, it's possible that he looked exactly like every metalwork teacher that has ever lived. But was he intelligent? Hard to say. I mean, how bright do you need to be to make a toffee hammer? And that's what he taught me to do. Well, was he mad, then? Again it's very difficult to tell. He did use to get a strange glint in his eye

every time anyone lit up a blowtorch. Perhaps he was secretly hoping they'd torch themselves to death. But there's nothing particularly peculiar or sinister in that. After all, very little else ever happened in the lessons, so we all used to look forward to the industrial accidents. No, I don't think that Mr Pargetter can tell us much about the

33

psyche of your average teacher. He was a pretty straight-forward person, really. A slightly greater than usual interest in metal, I suppose. But I always assumed that that was due to an iron deficiency.

Mr Evans: Woodwork teacher. Welsh. We called him Dai, mainly because we hoped he would. He had a very unusual

way of shortening lengths of wood. He would hit you across the bottom with them, and they would snap — sooner or later. It was also an interesting exercise to see which snapped first, the bending pupil or the wood. Mind you, now that corporal punishment has been more or less abolished in schools, he's probably retired. Or become a traffic warden. He was also president of the school rambling society. I joined this society mainly because there was this girl, you see . . . I secretly hoped that I'd get more chance to talk to her, out there on the open road. No such luck. She was a very fast walker. But the odd thing I noticed about Evans was that he was a completely different person outside school. Almost human. The same was true of . . .

Mr Jenkins: Geography. He, like Evans, was also Welsh. He, like Evans, also belonged to the rambling society. He, like Evans, also became a completely different person when exposed to fresh air. Ah! Maybe I've hit on something. Could it be that teachers are rather like gremlins? Give them fresh air and they're nice and friendly. Shut them in a classroom full of perfectly amiable children, willing to learn, and they become psychopathic maniacs. This was definitely what happened to Jenkins. Weren't we lucky that we didn't feed him after midnight, or splash him with water!

One thing I realised about both Jenkins and Evans was that they were not dedicated. Oh, they did their best. They hit us as often as possible, just to keep up the appearance of being good teachers. But there was no escaping the fact that were not committed teachers and they should have been — committed that is. I first realised that they were not the real McCoy while out rambling. Not once, *not once*, did Jenkins point into the sky and say: "Look! Cumulus nimbus!". That's just the sort of thing a geography teacher does all the time. Similarly, Evans never chopped down a tree and made a coffee table. And anyway, it's not possible to be both a rambler and a teacher, is it?

Perhaps they weren't teachers at all! There's a thought! Perhaps they were professional ramblers pretending to be teachers. But why? Who in their right mind would want to pretend to be a teacher? A teacher might, I suppose, but then I did say someone in their right mind. What could anyone possibly gain by pretending to be a teacher? I understand why people dress up and pretend to be gasmen. It's so that they can get into your house and steal your budgie. But why would anyone want to pretend to be a teacher? In order to get into the school? Maybe. But why? To steal something? What? There's nothing there! There aren't even enough pencils to go round! So, if Jenkins and Evans were not ramblers pretending to be teachers, maybe they were teachers pretending to be ramblers. Why? In order to get into Millets and steal a couple of anoraks? Ah! Yes! That sounds far more likely. An anorak is just the sort of thing a teacher would want to steal. After all, there's no way they could afford one on their salary. They'd be lucky to get a pacamac! Anyway, whatever the truth about these two Welshpersons, I gave up woodwork and geography and kept well clear of them.

Who else was there?

Mr Bloater: Maths and Games, but not at the same time! I say this because you were never quite sure. Mainly because he always smelt as though we were doing games. Not an unpleasant smell, just the honest perspiration that anyone builds up after ninety minutes' running aimlessly around a sports pitch, chasing a ball that's still being pumped up in

the groundsman's hut. But the problem was that he smelt like this during maths lessons, which tended to confuse some of our form who weren't very bright and had to rely on their sense of smell to work out what lesson they were in. Les Ash was regularly stripped and ready for showers before the rest of us got past the first logarithm. Mind you, he was never short of girlfriends, so it paid off!

Mr Bentley: English. He was also our form master. A man of high principle. Not that there's anything wrong with that. It seemed a bit of a waste of energy with us lot. One thing he did was to insist that we all wrote in exactly the same way. He spent much of our first year giving back work that didn't quite slope the right way, or didn't have a big enough squiggly bit on the capital "F". It was a bit of a pain at first, but eventually it proved a godsend because it meant that you could get other kids to do your homework for you! Brilliant! But did he realise that would happen? Or did he believe that we were above reproach? In short, was he stupid or devious?

Mr Homer: Chemistry. One of my chosen options for "O" level, a decision I still regret. Mainly because it has been of no use to me. I have never had occasion to mix dangerous chemicals together, not even to remove French mustard from a lapel. But that's what we learned to do. Mind you, you will realise as you slide along the razorblade of life that much of what you pick up at school (in the way of knowledge, that is, not rare tropical diseases) is of no use to

you whatsoever. Take algebra, for example. I can assure you right now (and I've been around, I can tell you) that there is *No such thing as algebra in the real world*. So there. And don't let anyone tell you there is. Certainly not a teacher. What do they know about anything?

Anyway, Mr Homer. I liked him. He'd obviously realised very early on that most of us would have no use at all for chemistry. Even the ones who eventually became international terrorists bought the ingredients at Tesco's (ready mixed). But what Homer did realise is that all kids like making a mess. And that's what we did for five years.

38

One particularly memorable day (according to my diary —
I don't remember it) was the day we did the experiment to
discover the boiling point of blood.

Like all good experiments, it required the use of a guinea
pig. Unfortunately, nobody had one. Oh, yes, Mark
Chapman had his Rottweiler with him. Such a trend-
setter, was Mark. He had a Rottweiler long before they
started being given away in the *Sun*. He even had one long
before Rottweilers started *writing* for the *Sun*. Anyway, the

dog was no good, since Francis & Fluffybits, "Purveyors of
Laboratory Equipment For Use in Schools and Colleges
since 1637" had so far not seen the need to produce a retort
large enough to house a Rottweiler, even a squashed-up
one. Surprising, really. You'd have thought that a large
firm like that would have attempted to move with the
times. After all, they had been "Suppliers of Bronchial
Inhalers To Minor Royalty". They even had a crest
embossed on each of their products. (I say "had been"
because they lost the contract under rather embarrassing
circumstances. Apparently a certain duke saw one of these
inhalers lying around on the dressing table of the Duchess
of Bent and, wondering what it was, sucked instead of
blowing, and got what he later described as a "ruddy great
gob-full" of Friars Balsam. He blamed the manufacturers
for not supplying adequate instructions, and Francis &

Fluffybits lost their very lucrative contract.) These days, of course, they have had to expand in order to survive, like the rest of us. They now even make those terrible little glass Bambis that you can win at fairs, if you're really unlucky.

Anyway, in those days they didn't make a retort large enough for our experiment, and so we were stumped. Or at least we would have been, if Miss Latex (Yes! That really was her name!) the French teacher hadn't walked into the lab at that precise moment. She had no real business there. It's just that she had popped in in order to avoid Mr Lurk, the physics teacher, who kept wanting to show her his invention. She was still crying, which was surprising because it was three hours since she'd last taught us. Anyway, it was handy that she turned up, as it happened. The details are slightly sketchy, but I know she said something about it making her blood boil, one thing led to another, and we completed the experiment. I can't exactly recall what conclusion we reached. It all got a bit confusing after the police turned up. Nobody actually called them, but they had got into the habit of making lightning raids on our school, especially when their arrest-rate was down.

Mind you, I think the local constabulary had got a vendetta against our school, which is odd because they used to be so friendly. They even came to the school and took the cycling proficiency lessons. Well, you couldn't expect a teacher to do it. They have no road sense. Have you ever seen one drive? Anyway, they stopped coming when Colin Butler failed his emergency stop. It wasn't his fault. He'd lent his brakes to Mickey Shorthouse. Sergeant Trotter was due to retire anyway. Looking on the bright side, Colin managed to hit Trotter's dog at the same time, so there were no grieving relatives left. Anyway, ever since then the police had really had it in for us. So you can probably realise what a field-day they had over the Pedley twins.

It was a biology lesson. We were doing an experiment to determine how identical identical twins are. Well, you can probably guess the rest. I've always maintained that it was their screams that alerted the police. I said as much in court. I was called as a character witness for Miss Portnoy, the biology teacher. I wasn't a lot of use, I'm afraid. All I could really tell the jury was that I thought she had lovely hair. Which she did. But I don't even know if it was a wig or not, because I had always been too shy to ask her if she was bald. Anyway, if I had asked her, it might have embarrassed her. I mean, she might not have known the answer. She probably would have done, being a biology teacher. Unlike Mr Bloater. I bet he didn't know whether he was wearing a wig or not. But then, maths was his subject. Maths and games, though not necessarily in that order.

Of the other teachers I basically remember very little. Of what they tried to teach me, I remember even less. But perhaps I shouldn't blame them too much. It was not entirely their fault. I mean to say, how could they teach me with any degree of efficiency? After all, most of them had not the slightest idea who the heck I was!

Love Miranda Bootle

It Takes All Types...

One thing that my research has shown me, apart from the inner secrets of many a caretaker's boiler-room, is this simple fact: Teacher-types are as many and varied as the little perforations in the average tea bag. And like the average tea bag, most teachers make a lousy cup of tea! However, in the interests of easy reference, I have sorted my findings into some sort of workable order. I have used Teacher-type headings, such as Angry, Bald, Cowardly, etc. I have then listed all of the relevant data under those headings. I hope this will make the types easier to identify, and subsequently avoid! The separate headings are:

Nature and habitat:
A description of the type of teacher, where to find them and a quick résumé of their habits, nasty or otherwise!

What to look out for:
The little tell-tale signs that will help you detect the Teacher-type, whether these signs be physical or (more likely) mental. This is useful from the point of view of knowing which ones to avoid!

What they teach:
Suggestions of the sorts of subject that would suit each type. Although all my research points to the strange-but-true fact that the subject taught rarely suits the teacher teaching it! You've probably already noticed this yourself!

What they say:
The sort of comment a particular type is likely to come out with.

What they mean:
What they actually *mean* by that comment!

Hobbies:
All work and no play makes Jack a dull boy. The same is true of teachers, although they obviously spend less time playing, which is why they are so dull!

How to cope:
Well, what it says, really! How to cope. How to avoid the pitfalls of each type of Teacher. Although, of course, it's not always possible!

What excuse will they buy?:
There are various situations that arise at school, when a good excuse for ndot doing something, or for not having done something, can be worth its weight in gold. Getting out of games, avoiding homework, failing to do homework, etc. Naturally, different situations require different excuses. Likewise different Teachers require different excuses. What washes with one doesn't even come vaguely clean with another!

Angry Teacher ......//

Nature and habitat:
This teacher type is very common indeed, although possibly more so in Secondary schools than in Primary. Consequently it can come as a bit of a shock when you first encounter this type. What is very obvious from the outset is the fact that this type is definitely angry. What is never clear is just precisely what they are angry *about*, which is odd, not to say disconcerting. After all, whenever you're angry you know why, don't you? There's usually a young brother or sister involved somewhere along the way. But that can't be why the teacher is screaming. They've probably never even met your brother. So just what exactly is making them yell so much? Well, it may surprise you to learn this, but all my research points to the fact that angry teachers are not actually angry about anything. It's even possible that they are not actually angry. Hard to accept, I know. Especially if you're on the receiving end. But it's true. So, why are they shouting? Well, they've been told that it's an essential part of pupil control.

What exactly is pupil control? Well, although the name suggests otherwise, it has nothing whatever to do with eyeballs. The fact that the screaming teacher's eyeballs are rotating at an impossibly high rate and one of them keeps popping out has nothing to do with anything — it's just an incidental by-product, and treatable with tablets. No, pupil control means getting the members of the class to behave in the way you want them to. To some teachers this comes naturally. They have a charm or charisma that enables them to control their class without an effort. OK, OK, so you've never met a teacher like that. But they do exist. Apparently. According to a NUT (Teacher's Union)

BEFORE...

DURING...

AFTER

45

report. Although I suppose they would say that, wouldn't they? However, given that the majority of teachers don't possess this quality, they have to fall back on their training. Training in pupil control offers the following options:

1) Making the subject interesting so that the pupils want to listen, even though their natural instinct may be to run around causing mayhem.
2) Bribery. This is not really a viable option, considering teachers' pay. It's more popular in the private sector.
3) Shouting. This is the third alternative and, quite frankly, the only viable one, given the impossibility of the other two. Certainly it's a popular choice. Be louder than anyone else so that your voice is heard above the others.

So what you mistook for bad temper on the part of your teacher is in fact skilful teaching. It doesn't make it any easier to put up with, but it's nice to know! So next time you get shouted at, just smile back. You've done nothing wrong. Your teacher is just practising the skills that he/she learned all those years ago at teacher training camp.

What to look out for:
You can spot an angry teacher straight away, because they look *Loud*!

What they teach:
Well, ideally they should be teaching games, where a nice loud voice and plenty of energy are needed. Of course life never works out like that, does it? The angry teacher usually ends up teaching religion.

What they say:
I'm not sure, but it sounds like:
"FUYRTM IJOI UY VXFDM, NLOIDCFDA!"

What they mean:
Again, I'm not sure, but I think they mean:
"FUYRTM IJOI UY VXFDM, NLOIDCFDA!"

Hobbies:
Anything that involves shouting and stamping. Many of them join the Territorials.

How to cope:
Earplugs.

What excuse will they buy?
Remember that they value their training. They remember everything that the Überstumbaumführer taught them at teacher training camp. Well, they had to. It was either that or have their nostrils cleaned with rusty barbed wire. This tends to make them rather traditional, so inventing long-winded explanations about rabid Rottweilers is a complete waste of time. A simple: "I forgot it" will suffice. But remember to insert the earplugs *before* you give the excuse!

Bald Teacher ...

Nature and habitat:

Found everywhere. It's a fact of life that large numbers of teachers go bald. Mostly men, but there have been many reported cases of bald female teachers. Why they should be reported beats me. It isn't an offence to be bald.

Baldness is supposedly a sign of either great intelligence or great virility. Or both. According to bald people it is, anyway. There are probably many advantages to being bald. No — can't think of any. I'm not bald, you see.

There are advantages and disadvantages to being bald if you're a teacher. The most obvious disadvantage centres around the pupils believing the myth about baldness. The part about being very intelligent, anyway. The poor teacher may be called upon to prove it, and then where would he be? The virility bit of the legend may well be true, although even that seems extremely unlikely. But intelligent? A teacher? Oh, come on! I wasn't born yesterday!

No, what we have here is a case of a bald person accidentally choosing the wrong profession (or being forced into it by a careers officer with a vendetta against baldies), or a person of average hair strength going into teaching and then going bald as a direct result. A sort of industrial accident. But how would that happen? How

STUDENT TEACHER

FORM TEACHER

HEAD OF DEPARTMENT

HEAD TEACHER

could a teacher go bald? Tension is known to be one of the major causes to hair loss. Put any kind of tension on hair and it will come out. Pulling it is a good way. That works fairly quickly, although obviously it's quite painful, especially if it's your own hair you're pulling. But then if you were pulling your own hair, your teachers wouldn't be the ones going bald, would they? And they are.

I think I've probably given you some clue as to how it's happening. What is maybe a little distressing is the fact that they may be blaming you behind your back. Hard to believe, I know, but true. Well, all I can say is don't feel guilty. It is not your fault. It's one of the problems with the job. Just as postmen can expect to get savaged to death by a couple of Scottie dogs regularly, so teachers can expect to find themselves pulling their own hair out. But you must not accept any blame or guilt. It's a simple scenario: they are teaching some particularly complex theoretical concept, like adding up, and you, quite understandably, don't understand a word of it. You start thinking that possibly you've turned up to a Spanish lesson by mistake. So what do you do? What would any intelligent teenager do? What have teachers spent the last X number of years drumming into you? That's right! Put your hand up and ask:

You: Excuse me, sir. Sorry to interrupt. But is this Spanish? Only I think I'm supposed to be in a maths lesson.

But instead of saying something reasonable like:

Teacher: No. You're all right. This is maths. You've no need to move classes, so you can stop pulling your wellingtons on.

Instead of saying something like that and letting us all know where we stand, what does the teacher do? Starts pulling out great tufts of hair. And, what is worse, giving you the distinct impression that it's in some way your fault.

What a cheek! I could understand the reaction if you had said something like:

You: I'm bored with this lesson now. Could you just tear out a great handful of what's left of your hair, please, sir?

But you didn't, did you?

There is an expression: "If you can't stand the heat, keep out of the kitchen." I had always assumed that it only applied to home economics teachers, but I think it probably applies across the board.

What to look out for:
Little trails of fallen hair. This can of course be especially useful if you have the same teacher next period, but in a different classroom. It means that you don't have to look up where you have to go in the timetable.

What they teach:
It seems unfair in a way, although they only have themselves to blame, but they tend to teach the really complicated things like spelling and sums. Why they don't switch to computer studies while they've still got enough hair to wrap over the top really beats me!

What they say:
"I think I'm going to lose my temper!"

What they mean:
"I know I'm going to lose more hair!"

Hobbies:
Strange though it may seem to you and me, they play an awful lot of sport. I suppose it's to work off some of the frustration and paranoia. Even stranger is the fact that they tend to choose sports that blow your hair about, which means they either have to suffer that wrap-over strand dangling in their eyes (which is always quite a useful

excuse for playing badly!) or wear a hairnet. The modern hairnet is, of course, virtually undetectable. Many famous sportspeople wear them to Olympic standard. And the more aggressive politicians were issued them when the decision to televise Parliament was taken. Neil Kinnock wears two.

How to cope:
Keep a little dustpan and brush handy.

What excuse will they buy?
Almost anything as long as you keep your eyes glued to the top of the bald teacher's head as you deliver it. You'll find that you've hardly started before they're waving you away with a "Yes, yes, yes! Get back to your seat!" If, however, your excuse fails, you can always fall back on the "is that a hairnet?" ploy, as in: "Sorry, but I've forgotten my games kit — is that a hairnet?" This is of course a bit below the belt — or can be, depending on how bad the hair loss has got!

SPOT THE TEACHER

Cowardly Teacher

Nature and habitat:
Found in cupboards. They occasionally venture out into the classroom, but only to tell the class that they are needed back in the cupboard (the teacher, not the whole class! It's not big enough!). But what exactly are they doing in there?

It's none of your business — get on with your work! No. OK. I'll tell you what they're doing in that cupboard — nothing. Yep, that's right. Nothing. Well, it's not strictly true. I mean to say, it's impossible to do nothing. Even when you're in total repose, you're breathing. If you're not breathing you're dead. But even if you're dead you're doing something. You're lying down, perfectly still. Although that does depend on how you died. You could be folded double inside a black plastic bin liner. And likewise the teacher in the cupboard is not doing nothing. Hello! That's a double negative, isn't it? Is it grammatically correct? I'll ask a teacher, if I can find one who knows.

What the teacher in the cupboard is actually doing is hiding. Yep, that's about it. Hiding. Hiding from the class. What the heck for? Did they ever do him/her any harm? Have they ever refused to do homework? Failed to turn up? Laughed openly at his/her teaching methods? All pretended to be from a different planet and spoken in a strange language? Removed any of the teacher's vital organs except by accident or in the interests of medical experimentation? No! Definitely not! So what is the teacher afraid of? Certainly not being set upon physically. This teacher's got black belts in Ludo, Judo and Cluedo, so that's not their problem. No. Their problem is fear of being asked to teach.

What to look out for:
Who knows? Unless you actually take a polaroid of this teacher on one of their rare appearances, you won't really have any idea what you're looking for. In fact some of these teachers are so rare you can get stickers that say: "I've seen the Head of Year at Farn Street Comprehensive."

What they teach:
As little as possible! But unfortunately when they do teach it's always one of the basic subjects, like English or maths. It's never something obscure like Dutch. Which is probably why the Government keeps saying: "We must get more teachers into the classroom." This is obviously political jargon for "We must get more teachers out of the cupboard."

What they say:
"Has everyone got a pencil?"

What they mean:
"I want to get back in the cupboard."

Hobbies:
Since they don't like to be recognised, and certainly don't want people to know that they're a teacher, they like anything that involves a fair amount of dressing-up and disguising: amateur theatricals, transvestism, Morris dancing — that sort of thing.

How to cope:
So long as they stay in the cupboard, there's no problem. However, if you think there's a danger that they might accidentally venture out, the only answer is to fit a lock. A standard padlock may be satisfactory, although total security can only really be achieved by using a combination lock. To be doubly sure, make certain that the only person in the school who knows the combination is really stupid (*see* **Dunce Teacher**).

What excuse will they buy?
A tap on the cupboard door and a "Would you like to see what our cat has done to (or on) my homework?" works every time!

Dunce Teacher...

Nature and habitat:

It may surprise you to learn (this book is meant to be a learning experience, but it still may surprise you to learn) that there are a large number of dunce teachers. By that I don't mean teachers of dunces, although obviously there are some of those as well. I'm actually referring to teachers who are not very bright. So how do they become teachers? It's not as difficult as you might imagine. They join the wrong queue at the Social Security office, and instead of getting a disability pension for an old badminton injury, they get offered the post of Head of English at a large comprehensive. It's called beurocratic error, except that they spell it properly!

It happened to me. I was very small at the time, but I remember it as if it were forty-odd years ago. My mum had taken me with her to the clinic to get some National Health orange juice, and by some slip of a pen I got offered up for adoption. It's easily done. Give my mother her due, she did adopt me. Some mothers would have just walked out and left me. I just hope she's never regretted the decision. I still show my gratitude in little ways. For instance I always get her slippers for her in the evening. Although now that we live about three hundred miles apart I have to post them. Still, blood is thicker than water, as I discovered at school as a by-product of the Pedley experiment (*see* p.40).

But, having got into the job by accident, why don't they get back out of it if they're not suited to it? Well, yes, that would be the smart thing to do. Which is precisely why they don't do it! They're not smart, remember? So they stay in the job. Getting by, somehow. Busking their way along. And some of them become surprisingly good at it. The others get promotion!

What to look out for:
A blank expression. This is usually a dead giveaway. But be careful, because deep thought often looks exactly the same as vacuousness. So the teacher you're writing off as a dunce could be very intelligent. Although, of course, that's very unlikely!

What they teach:
They're not sure, so don't ask them. If you do ask: "What do you teach?", you're likely to get the answer: "Children."

What they say:
"Could you all hold up your text books, please?"

What they mean:
"I need to be reminded what a book looks like."

Hobbies:
"What are they?"

56

How to cope:
Walk around with a copy of some intellectual-looking book or magazine sticking out of your pocket. That will keep this teacher-type at bay. *Astrophysics Now!* would be a good choice. *The Bumper Book of Sun Crosswords* wouldn't. Oh, I don't know though!

What excuse will they buy?
If you start your excuse with a really long word, like "unfortunately", the dunce teacher will need no further excuse. In fact, they will be unable to *cope* with any further excuse!

Educated Teacher

Nature and habitat:

Well, this is a tricky one, because in a way "educated" and "teacher" are almost contradictory terms. You see, you don't need to be educated in order to teach. Any more than you need to be a lumberjack to know what a tree is. On the other hand, you can't be completely stupid. You have to be something in between. Stupid in an educated sort of way. Because teaching is a conveying of knowledge, not a test of how clever you are. It's a common mistake, made by pupils and teachers alike. Very often the highly educated person makes a very bad teacher, because they get frustrated by the lesser intelligence of their pupils. By the same token, of

course, the very stupid teacher gets frustrated by the higher intelligence of *their* pupils. But then, I can see that would be very annoying. Especially in Infants school.

Of course, some of these highly educated teachers revel in their superior knowledge. We had a teacher at my school who used to say: "Let's recapitulate," just to see the blank expressions cross our faces. Unfortunately for him Sniffer Lacey was slightly deaf. This was the result of sticking a pencil in his ear. Another teacher had told him that he was empty-headed, and he wanted to see if this was true. Anyway, because of this he misheard, thought the educated teacher had said "let's decapitate" and . . . well, it was another day off and a trip to church. But not before some of the older boys had performed an autopsy as part of their Queen's Scout Badge. Do you know, the interesting thing was that that brain, for all its great thoughts, didn't look any different from an ordinary person's brain. Or taste any different, apparently. Yet more proof that education is a dangerous thing!

What to look out for:
A superior look. Nose in the air. But be careful. You may see a new teacher walking around with their nose high in the air, and think to yourself: "Oh, no! Not another flippin' intellectual!" But you might be wrong. It might just be the fact that they haven't quite got used to the smell of the school yet!

What they teach:
Nothing that ordinary mortals like you or I could possibly understand. But don't stop them to ask for a translation, or they'll lose their train of thought and have to go right back to the beginning!

What they say:
In my experience it's usually: "Let's recapitulate," followed shortly afterwards by: "Aaargh!"

What they mean:
I have about as much idea as Sniffer Lacey did.

Hobbies:
Anything that sounds less pretentious than it is, such as neo-classical jazz concertos played on old mountain bike-frames by ageing hippies wielding lightly poached kippers. Miss it and weep!

How to cope:
If you want to avoid this teacher, then look stupid. This can be achieved with practise. Some of you may be amazed just how easy it is! However, if you want to engage in conversation with this teacher, wear glasses. They're suckers for glasses. This is handy to know if you want to make sure someone else gets lumbered talking to this teacher-type.

What excuse will they buy?
Hardly anything, I'm afraid. You could try the "anguished intellectual" approach. You know the sort of thing: "I really struggled to do my homework last night, sir (or miss), but you know the Muse just was not upon me." It won't work, but it's worth a try!

Flash teacher —

Nature and habitat:
You must have seen them. Or heard their car. Or been
dazzled by their jacket. Or fallen about laughing at them at
the school disco. Generally male, although there is a female
version, the flash teacher seems to want everyone to believe
they are a minor popstar, rather than the teacher of
something unpronounceable at a local secondary school.
Consequently they are always in debt, as they desperately
pursue fashion in clothes, cars, music, everything. Not that
they are fooling anyone, except themselves. They are at
their worst when the student teachers turn up for practice.
They start arriving early, wearing aftershave that smells
like a domestic cleanser that makes little graphic taps curl
up in TV adverts, and whistling in the corridors, as if
they're trying to say: "Look, I know I look young enough
to be a pupil, but I'm actually a teacher, and to prove it I'm
whistling in the corridor without getting told off!". Very
clever! Let them try dropping a bit of litter in the
playground when the caretaker's got his hearing-aid
turned up! Eh? Eh? Oh, yes! He'll soon have them
whistling in a different pitch!

   The worst thing these flash teachers do when there's
someone around to impress is to start teaching! Yeah!
Unbelievable, I know! But true! They prepare lessons.
They do all the things they spent two years at teacher
training camp learning, and the last five years of professional teaching forgetting. So suddenly you're having to
learn things in class, just so sir can look good in the eyes of
some nubile student teacher who — if she's half as bright
as she looks — will already have sussed that he's a complete
Rodney anyway. Babycham after school? You've gotta be
joking, mate!

   But while this silly game of cat and mouse is going on,
you're being forced to learn. And that can be a real culture
shockd, as you sit there thinking: what happened to the

usual lessons? He may be flash, but his usual lessons are great. His usual routine for a forty-minute period went:

FIRST TEN MINUTES:Trying to remember what happened last time. Then the discovery that the most rivetting thing that took place during the previous lesson was Les Ash's admission that he'd got spam sandwiches for lunch again. Not again! His granny must have been stock-piling since the War.

NEXT TEN MINUTES: Usually the most difficult to fill, because it's decision time for sir. He has to decide what to teach, based on information received about what he taught last time. Les could usually be counted on to help out here too. It can take a good ten minutes to examine two rounds of spam sandwiches in order to determine whether they are as "spammy" as yesterday's or not. On a good day Les could usually retrieve one of yesterday's from behind the radiator, so that an accurate comparison could be made. In fact, since the school went over to contract cleaners and the caretaker's duties were reduced to moaning, torturing first years, and fattening up the school pets for experimentation, you could usually find anything up to twenty sandwiches in varying stages of decay behind the radiator.

NEXT TEN MINUTES: Halfway through the lesson, and it's as good a time as any to discuss what's hot and what's not on the music scene. I wonder if the class realise that Mr Flash is taking notes? If they did they might be tempted to say: "Freddy and the Dreamers are making a comeback, sir."

LAST TEN MINUTES: Well, hardly worth starting anything now. Sometimes there's a half-hearted effort to get the books out, usually preceded by a very genuine effort to try and remember what the lesson is supposed to be. This is usually abandoned in favour of a quick check to make sure everyone has a copy of the textbook for next time, just in case. Followed by a quick check that everyone actually knows what the textbook they're supposedly using looks like. Followed by a quick check that everyone actually knows what a *book* looks like. Then there's just a few seconds left for the "shall I/shan't I set homework?", plus the decision to set homework, but to tell everyone not to bother to hand it in. Then it's the bell, and a very slow walk past the fifth form common room on the way back to the staff room, where it's his turn to make the tea.

What to look out for:
Anything that's ten years or more out of date. You can be sure that Flash will be wearing it. He's the only teacher on the staff to drive a customised Lada.

What they teach:
Well, by rights it should be something like liberal studies, politics, or whatever's going to disappear in the next round of cutbacks. But it never is. It's always English. Which is a pity because he teaches it very badly, peppering his conversation with bits of French!

What they say:
"Could you all hold your textbooks up, please?"

What they mean:
"I want to see what I'm supposed to be teaching."

Hobbies:
Customising their Lada. Trying to walk in flares and cuban heels. Tinting their hair. Watching at discos (too old to dance without getting thrown out!).

How to cope:
There's really not much to cope *with*, as long as you turn up fairly regularly.

What excuse will they buy?
Ah! This is different. Don't make the mistake of trying to appeal to them on their own level. Don't, for instance, say: "I haven't done my homework because I couldn't be bothered." They won't understand that, because they think they're being "laid-back", not lazy. Instead you could try the "It was too hard" approach. The teacher won't want to take the trouble to explain it, and you'll be off the hook! But be careful. Don't keep using this one, or you might get sent down a set, to a far less understanding teacher-type!

Genuine Teacher...

Nature And habitat:
A rare breed, but they do exist, honestly. This teacher genuinely wants to pass on knowledge, despite their pupils' unwillingness to learn, despite regularly being set on fire, despite every daily hazard they're forced to suffer. Even despite the fact that nobody among the rest of the staff likes them. They have a mission: to spread the word. And no-one is going to stop them.

"But why are they unpopular with the rest of the staff?" I hear you cry. "If they're such good teachers," you continue to bleat, "why aren't they loved and cherished?" Because they give the game away, that's why! You know as well as I do that it only takes one person getting an answer right in a test to make the rest of you look stupid. If everyone gets the answer wrong, then the test can be judged fairly on the basis of who is rightest. But if someone is actually correct, that screws up the entire system. And the same applies to teaching. It only takes one bad apple to do it properly, and before you know where you are, kids'll be running home telling their parents that they've learned something, making the parents feel less intelligent, and generally upsetting the status quo. No, perish the thought! It makes me shudder just to think about it. After all, you don't go to school to learn — it's a halfway house between birth and work.

What to look out for:
Spotting a genuine teacher is really quite easy. There's a glint in the eye that says: "I am genuinely interested in what you are saying. I value your opinion." This is the point at which to take avoiding action, unless you want to wind up well and truly educated.

What they teach:
Again of course they're wasted. They tend to teach one of the options that everyone drops at the first possible opportunity. Like music or Latin.

What they say:
"Hmm . . . fascinating!"

What they mean:
"Hmm . . . fascinating!"

Hobbies:
Rambling. On, and on, and on, and on . . .

How to cope:
A good ploy, during a private tuition session, is to suddenly start talking in complete gobbledegook. This throws them long enough for you to pretend to kill yourself. This will cause them to call an ambulance, during which time you can quickly assume a disguise. Don't run away, because they'll know you've done it, and you'll never hear the last of it. A disguise is good because, although they'll probably realise that it's still you, they won't want to tackle you about it in front of a complete stranger (you in disguise). The other thing to remember is to make sure that it really is gobbledegook. Don't cut corners by using a genuine foreign language. Chances are this teacher has been to most countries on fact-finding holidays, and speaks every language on the planet.

What excuse will they buy?
Anything, as long as it's said with real feeling and sounds genuine. But practise. Sounding genuine is not a thing that comes naturally to most people.

Harassed teacher

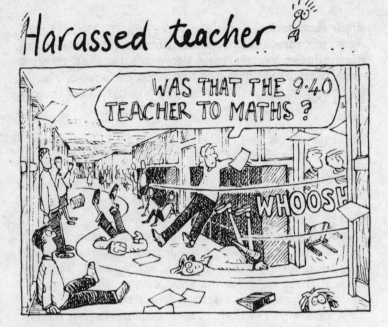

Nature and habitat:

They're not easily found. This is not because they're rare, but because they're never where they should be, which is also why they're harassed. They move from lesson to lesson like a typhoon, arriving where they should have been before they left, which is where they should be now. No, they don't understand it either! There's no point in referring to the timetable. They're using that to wedge up the corner of the desk, and the only way to use it would be to remember which room their desk is in.

Don't be fooled. They are not absent-minded. They haven't got time to be. So why do they teach? They don't know. Oh, they'll tell you that it looked easy when they were at school, so they thought they'd give it a go. But that's not the real reason. The real reason probably has more to do with them making a series of wrong turnings on

the highway of life. Cor! That's deep, isn't it? What I mean
is that they know they're perfectly cut out to be something,
but they can't remember what it is. So while they try to
remember, they teach. Oh, don't get me wrong. They're
not bad at it. I mean, they're very popular. Well, they get
the sympathy vote, anyway.

What to look out for:
If they're in the vicinity, just look out!

What they teach:
Nothing, really. They're never in one place long enough. If
they were, it would probably be something that required
huge numbers of text and reference books.

What they say:
"Er — what?"

What they mean:
"Who on earth are you?"

Hobbies:
Don't be silly!

How to cope:
Avoid school corridors, and any other places of access
between classrooms, during change-overs between lessons.
That way you may also avoid a head-on collision!

What excuse will they buy?
Most things. But keep it very short, otherwise it's unlikely
that they'll hear it. Then they'd have to stop and come back
and get you to repeat it, which would have two side effects,
one pleasant, and one unpleasant. They are:

1) the change of direction would totally confuse them and
you might not see them for weeks;
2) they would listen carefully to your excuse and then not
believe you.

I feel sure you can work out which is which!

Interested Teacher.

Nature and habitat:
Found in many a classroom. "Great!" I hear you cry. Well, yes. Maybe. At least it can be. Unfortunately, the thing they're interested in is rarely the thing they're teaching you at that particular moment. There they are, happily teaching away, not causing any trouble or annoyance to anyone trying to sleep, when suddenly they go: "Ah! That's interesting!", sit down and start reading. This obviously leaves the class in some doubt as to how to proceed. Saying "What is, miss (or sir)?" has no effect. Throwing things has no effect. Even Mark Chapman whipping out his chainsaw and starting it up just gets a very cursory "Put that away before you kill somebody," without the teacher even looking up from the book. Even if Chapman doesn't turn it off immediately, all the reaction this causes is: "Oh, all right! Kill somebody first, but then put it away!" And still without looking up.

What can be so fascinating that it takes the teacher away from the task of imparting knowledge? Who knows! The only thing you can be sure of is that they're not going to tell *you*. Oh, no! You've got to make do with the usual old boring stuff. The stuff that's virtually impossible to remember because it's so dreary that even Norris McWhirter doesn't know it. The stuff that contestants on the *64,000 Dollar Question* specialise in. The stuff that taxi drivers win *Mastermind* with.

It's amazing, isn't it? If you started reading in class when the teacher was trying to talk to you, you'd really be for it! Even if it was something much more interesting, like *JACKIE*. It's so unfair, isn't it? Still, as I've told you before, life is rarely fair.

What to look out for:
This type of teacher is very easy to spot. You'll hear something that sounds like "Ah!", then all you'll see for

the rest of the lesson is the top of their head. One consolation is that this new-found piece of knowledge might just make them a better teacher — but don't hold your breath!

What they teach:
Unfortunately, as luck would have it (or more properly as bad luck would have it), they tend to teach the more interesting subjects. But they keep the best bits to themselves.

What they say:
"Ah!"

What they mean:
I never found out. They were too busy reading to tell me!

Hobbies:
Gathering useless bits of information, such as . . . ah!

How to cope:
Accept that they are like they are, and try to jot down the titles of the books they're reading. That way you might learn something!

What excuse will they buy?
Anything long and boring. Never try them with an excuse that starts: "You'd never guess what happened to my homework on the way to school this morning!", because that sort of thing sounds exciting. (OK, it doesn't sound exciting to you, but these are teachers we're dealing with, remember? Their idea of excitement is a Rusty Lee cookery item, or a Les Dennis game show.)

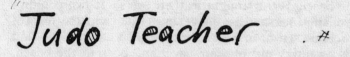

Judo Teacher

Nature and habitat:

One of the many extra-curricular activities that schools sometimes offer is judo. For those who have never heard of it, basically it consists of someone thick as a brick trying to prove that they're also stronger than one. However, it's enormously popular and is a useful skill if you ever want to get a job riding shotgun on a milkfloat.

But what sort of people teach it? Well, in the real world it's usually taught by muscle-bound short blokes who were once weedy short blokes until they finally got fed-up with having sand kicked in their face. They took this as a personal insult, although the truth was that it was usually accidental. You see, them being so short, the sand (flicked up by passers-by wearing those silly beach flip-flops that no-one would be seen dead wearing anywhere other than the beach) went straight in their eye(s). It just couldn't avoid it, since sand has not yet been fitted with any form of direction sensor or homing device. If it had it could find it's own way out of your navel and back to the beach. Anyway, poor old Weedy was faced with two choices. Walk along with his eyes shut, or go to the Isle of Wight for his holidays. But then he'd get pebbles flicked up in his face. Weedies can't win. There was a third alternative. Learn judo. It didn't keep the sand away but it helped him bear the pain.

So is the person who teaches judo in schools a sand-flicked beach weedy? Not usually. Usually it's the person you'd least expect to find teaching such an aggressive sport. Like Mr Sponter, that little chap who comes in twice a week to teach the fifth form poetry appreciation. Up until then, their idea of poetry was "There was a young fella from Cosham", etc! Now they can proudly say: "This is a good poem. It rhymes and everything!" But, once the poetry is over and the books are closed, Sponter takes off his glasses (and the cord keeping them around his neck), folds them neatly away in their case, unfolds and dons his judo suit and neatly ironed orange belt, and suddenly he's no longer Eric Sponter — he's a martial arts warrior from the ancient orient! And that's probably why he does it. But there may be another reason. What is the meaning of that macabre grin that flickers across his face as he watches the pupils in his care half-killing (and occasionally full-killing) each other? I think we should be told!

What to look out for:
Anyone could be a closet judo teacher. It's as hard to spot one as it is to spot a Ninja creeping up on you until you're standing there with your head in the floor looking up at you.

What they teach:
Judo, obviously.

What they say:
"Remember the ancient disciplines!"

What they mean:
"Pull his head off!"

Hobbies:
Butterfly collecting. It's not really the collecting bit — it's the pinning the things to bits of board afterwards that they really get into. When they're not doing that they like building little walled flowerbeds, so that they can break the bricks with the side of their hands.

How to cope:
Avoid invitations to poetry appreciation lessons!

What excuse will they buy?
If you do find yourself in their judo class, and you survive long enough to go back for more but then chicken out, don't try using the "I forgot my kit" ploy. It works on normal teachers, but not Mr Sponter. He'll just say: "Do it in your underwear!", and you probably will, right there and then!

Kind Teacher

Nature and habitat:

My favourite type! Be gentle with me, teacher! I'm not very bright! This type of teacher is usually found in primary schools, although very occasionally one escapes into the big bad world of secondary education. They look like everybody's favourite aunt. Big, cuddly, with a large bust, woolly cardy and tweed skirt. And that's just the men! Only joking! I've never known a single male teacher who dressed like that. Or a married one. Except on weekends and then only in the privacy of Beckenham High Street.

The female version of the kind teacher looks like that. She's always there when you need help with your reading. Always there when you've lost your PE vest. Always there when you fall over in the playground. That's a point! She

BAFF!

OOPS-A-DAISY! I'D BETTER GET THE WINTERGREEN

is, isn't she? The minute you fall, she's at your elbow. Perhaps it was her that pushed you. What a thought! I do hope not! It would destroy my little bit of faith in the state education system. I might even stop trying to retake my 11-plus.

The male version of this teacher is no less caring. He's middle-aged, homely, balding, bespectacled. Just the sort of chap you'd run a mile from if you saw him hanging around in the park.

But this type of teacher is wonderful. They make learning so easy. Not that I'm convinced that they teach very much, but you seem to learn anyway.

What to look out for:
Anything that looks like a bundle of old clothes, taking themselves off to Oxfam. There's a very kindly old teacher in there somewhere. Don't prod too hard — they may be asleep.

What they teach:
They are good all-rounders, but don't let them near the school computer, unless of course you want to blow it up.

What they say:
"That's lovely, dear!"

What they mean:
"What is it?"

Hobbies:
Brass rubbing, stroking cats, applying Wintergreen ointment.

How to cope:
There's no need to "cope". Just sit back and enjoy it!

What excuse will they buy?
Any excuse will be acceptable, as long as it's said in a sad little voice. Tears, if you can manage them, are always a big hit.

Loud Teacher...

Nature and habitat:
Don't confuse this type with the angry teacher. This teacher is not shouting at you. Well, they are, but not for the same reasons as the angry teacher. Although of course it all sounds much the same to your poor ears. So why are they shouting? I can think of three possible reasons:

1) they're so pleased with their knowledge of their subject, that they want to shout it from the rooftops;
2) they're so unsure of their knowledge of their subject that they feel they need to shout in order to stop anyone daring to question their authority;

3) they are deaf.
Oh. I've thought of a fourth:
4) they're mad.

Well, I think we can dismiss (4) on the grounds that we've already agreed that all teachers are a little mad anyway. What about (3)? Well, I think you'd know if they were deaf. They'd probably say "pardon" a lot. Which would suggest deafness. Or wind. So the truth is either (2) or (1). And I think that that's probably about as close as you'll ever get to the truth.

What to look out for:
There are no tell-tale visual signs connected with this teacher type. The signs are more aural. It's more what you hear than what you see. You can hear this teacher clearly from the other end of the school.

What they teach:
Unfortunately, it's always something best taught quietly — something you don't really want the rest of the school to know you're learning. Like sex. Or algebra.

What they say:
"That's a buttock!"

What they mean:
Well, assuming that they actually *do* know what they're talking about, they probably mean exactly what they say. Teachers can be amazingly literal sometimes. However, if they don't know what they're talking about, then your guess is as good as mine. But if they don't know what they're talking about, then they're probably holding the picture upside down, anyway!

Hobbies:
Public speaking (or public yelling), amateur theatricals (they aren't very good but everyone can hear them), and

auctioneering (let's hope they don't hold the things upside down there!).

How to cope:

You could try cottonwool balls in your ears, but then you might miss a bit of interesting information. The best thing to do is to persuade your parents to move nearer the school. That way you can attend this teacher's lessons without getting out of bed!

What excuse will they buy?

Well, given their penchant for loudness, try to avoid any sort of excuse that involves intimate details. For example, although loud teachers don't usually take games, it's not unheard of. So if you want to avoid games *and* acute embarrassment at the same time, one of the following excuses should *not* be used:

a) "I have a very unpleasant growth in the Private Sector."
b) "I've forgotten my kit."

Can you work out which one not to use? I feel sure you can!

Music (al) Teacher ♪♫

Nature and habitat:
Found in the music room, mostly. Tinkling on the piano during breaks. Sorry. Let me rephrase that. Tinkling *with* the piano during breaks. Of course, there are a variety of different types of music teacher. There's the teacher at junior school who offers to run the school orchestra. This is usually the least musically talented, or most deaf, member of staff. You see, deafness is a definite plus for running a junior orchestra. Because of the noise. Sorry, I mean the music. You see, there's a feeling that the "youngsters" (whatever they are) should be allowed time to find their way around their instrument. What? The triangle? It's got three sides, all of them identical. The only way you can tell it's the right way up is if it doesn't fall off the string when you hit it. And what about the recorder?

When I die and go to Hell, I'm going to ask for the *Up To Your Neck In Camel Diarrhoea Punishment*. I'll even settle for the *Having Your Horoscope Forecast Daily By Russell Grant Punishment*. Anything to avoid the *Recorder Punishment*. I was told about this by a friend who died, went to Hell, but got sent back to earth for changing channels during "Neighbours". He told me about the *Recorder Punishment*. It consists of spending eternity having to listen to six eight-year-old girls with ribbons in their long blond hair, plasters on their knees and braces on their teeth playing *Lord of The Dance* followed by *Morning Has Broken* on recorders. They only play the tunes through once, but it takes an eternity. *Morning Has Broken* on the recorder! I now know why Cat Stevens renounced pop music and turned to Islam. He heard six girls playing his greatest hit on recorders.

81

But secondary school music teachers are strange animals. Get them in the classroom, and they behave as though no-one has written a decent bit of music since Henry VIII got some sixteenth-century Rod Argent to ghost-write *Greensleeves*, and then put his own name to it. But ask them to be musical director of the school's annual production of *The Mikado*, and they rearrange it so that it sounds like The Pogues. And you just wait till you see what they wear in the "pit" during performances. Julian Clary eat your heart out!

What to look out for:
The male music teacher might have his hair slightly longer than the rest of the staff. The female music teacher might have hers slightly shorter than the rest of the staff. Except the bald ones. Unless, of course, she's bald herself. But it's the lapel badge that gives them away — "Keep Music Live." And naturally they have a large record collection to go with it.

What they teach:
Muzak. Sorry, music. No! I was right the first time.

What they say:
"*They Might Be Giants* has no coherent musical structure."

What they mean:
"I have never heard of *They Might Be Giants*."

Hobbies:
Male: Tinkering with obscure musical instruments. Trying to get a tune out of virtually anything. Their burning ambition is to appear on *That's Life!*, playing *Amazing Grace* on a Flymo.
Female: Attending obscure musical events. But she would also like to appear on *That's Life!*, getting a tune out of something strange (although Esther Rantzen would only

allow it if the instrument were a vegetable of rude anatomical shape).

How to cope:
Buy a really old musical instrument. Something that hasn't been seen around for years, but something that causes your grandad to say: "Oh! We all used to play them, you know! It's what won us the war". (Obviously he won't say that if he's German. He'll probably say something about coming second.) Anyway, take the instrument into school and ask the music teacher to show you how to play it. It'll keep them happy for months. Oh! A word of warning. Make sure that it's really dirty, otherwise you might find yourself having to take a lesson. On the other hand, if it's really grubby, it's going to take the teacher so long to get it into mint condition that you'll probably have left the school. Making sure it's got a little bit missing should ensure the success of this plan.

What excuse will they buy?
It depends what you're trying to avoid. One excuse that will never work with this teacher is: "I'm tone deaf!" It rarely matters to them, as they never really expect the music made by a group of schoolkids to sound anything like the real thing. This is probably also why they fail to appreciate pop, because it's played by people who, in their estimation, are too young to be able to do it properly. What they fail totally to appreciate is that many of the groups *are* doing it properly. They *intend* to sound like that.

Love Miranda Bootle

Nasty Teacher . . . .

Nature and habitat:
You're probably going to say: "Oh, yes! I know dozens of these!" And possibly you do. But they're not as common-place as you may believe. In fact, they're not even as commonplace as teachers would *like* you to believe. Because many of the teachers who appear to be nasty are not like that at all. Well, perhaps a little bit.

Of course the nasty teachers of years ago are legends. Like the maths master who could decapitate a child at twenty metres with a rolled-up ball of A4 paper. Or the biology teacher who kept the local hospital supplied with kidneys and other organs, kindly "donated" by children who had forgotten their homework. Then there was Mrs Box, the Home Economics teacher who microwaved the entire third year. At first she got a lot of sympathy.

"What an unfortunate accident!" everyone said, until it was discovered that she had a degree in electrical engineering! In fact, she was never without a bit of fuse wire, just in case the opportunity arose to reduce classroom overcrowding.

Mind you, classrooms were very crowded in those days. I heard of one class that was so packed with pupils that they went without a teacher for four years. Fortunately nobody noticed. In fact it didn't really come to light until the following year, when they had a teacher, and exam grades suddenly shot up. One of the pupils passed an "O" level (only 'N' grade, but they called it a pass). This caused questions to be asked in corridors of the local Education Authority. Questions were even heard being asked in the staffroom. Questions like: "Was it tea you wanted, or coffee?"

Oh, yes! You could see that the teachers were really worried. After all, the coffee was running out. Thank heavens for teachers like Mrs Box, they used to say. Until she tried out one of her patent truth drugs on a few members of staff, prior to using it in class. Unfortunately none of those staff members will ever tell the truth again. Not that they told the truth much in the past, but now they wouldn't even lie convincingly, unless it was in a coffin. Poor Mrs Box. Her teacher's natural inquisitiveness and desire for experimentation was finally her undoing. She had only developed the truth drug so that she could determine whether her class knew the answers to questions she asked them, or whether they were playing her up. If only she'd realised. They were all too scared of her to play her up. Still, she should be out soon, but whether she'd be able to adjust to the GCSE or not is another matter. She'd certainly miss the gratuitous corporal punishment. Still, she'd enjoy the classroom violence that's replaced it.

These days of course it's very difficult to be a genuinely nasty teacher. I mean, physical violence is out. Mind you, in some schools the kids have cut out the middle man and started hitting each other. Some kids even hit themselves, which is energy-conserving and therefore more environmentally friendly. But if the teacher can't hit you, what can they do? Shout at you? Yes, I suppose so. But what would they shout? Something like: "I won't hit you in a minute, if you keep doing that!"? Very frightening. It'd make me sit up, I can tell you! Ah, sarcasm! That has always been the good old teacher stand-by. The trouble is that it loses its impact when no-one understands it, and you have to start explaining it. Which is why some teachers are very keen for you to learn some big long words. It's not because they want to improve your vocabulary — it's because they want to use the long words to humiliate you in front of the rest of the class!

What to look out for:
This type is harder to detect than in previous years. Gone is the facial scar, the cat-o'-nine-tails and the electric cattle prod, only to be replaced with a smarmy smile. If you suspect your teacher of being a secret nasty, ask them, as subtly as possible, if their clothes are blood-proof. If they say "yes", it's a bit of a giveaway!

What they teach:
To their great disappointment, they rarely teach the

subjects where pupil accidents are an everyday occurrence, like games, gymnastics, etc. I mean, nobody even looks up from the *Sun* crossword if the gym teacher walks into the staffroom saying: "We really should get those wallbars fixed. They've just come off again, crushing the whole of 3b this time." No. These teachers usually teach things like English language. And, even though the pen is mightier than the sword, there have been very few reported cases of entire classrooms being wiped out by one. It's also unlikely for an English teacher to be able to get away with saying:

"What happened was, you see . . . Nobbitts Junior couldn't spell kalashnikov (neither can I!), so I took one into class, just to help him. Unfortunately the safety catch was off, and . . ."

No. He'd never get away with it. But where there's a will, there's a way, so watch out!

What they say:
"Oh, hello!"

What they mean:
"Oh! You're still with us, then! I must bribe the cooks to increase the dosage!"

Hobbies:
Clay pigeon shooting without the clay; wargaming (but only if they can bring their own weapons) and school trips!

How to cope:
Wear a bullet/bomb/sarcasm-proof jacket. Bribe or bully a smaller child (or ask a dunce teacher) to be your personal school dinners taster. If they eat your dinner and die, make sure you don't eat the bit they've just spat out. It could be poisonous. Take sandwiches. Stay at home.

What excuse will they buy?
Don't be a complete Rodney!

Optimistic teacher

Nature and habitat:

It's a sad fact but true that there are some school kids who simply don't take to education. They are to learning what Timmy Mallett is to peace and quiet. Or talent. They just can't cut it, however hard they try. In a way they provide a natural outlet for teacher frustration. Teachers can be as sarcastic as they like, because the child doesn't realise they're doing it. In the old days these children were useful because they were totally indestructible and didn't bruise very easily. These are the kids who get labelled dunce, no-hoper, complete Rodney, etc. They are one of the few topics of conversation in the staffroom, apart from football, badminton, and "What's four down: 'Flightless Australian bird, E something U'?" It usually goes like this:

> "I had the pleasure of teaching Mandy Scoggins today."
> (*Numerous Groans. A lone voice says*):
> "Who's she?"
> "She's in your form."
> "Oh."

There then follows a long general discussion about Mandy Scoggins' abilities, lack of abilities, chances of survival in the real world.

> "Wouldn't it be kinder to get the caretaker to put her down now?"

Then, from somewhere in the corner, where someone is taking their turn to do the washing up, a lone voice:

> "I like Mandy Scoggins."

Actually this person isn't taking their turn to do the

washing up. They're taking someone else's turn. Not that anyone notices. The only teacher who understands the rota is away. Anyway, this teacher doesn't mind doing someone else's washing up, any more than they mind having to defend Mandy Scoggins. For this person is an *optimistic teacher*.

General consternation. Cries of:
"What!?"
"You've got to be joking!"
"She can't even hold a pencil!"
"She can," defends the optimist.
"Not the right way round!"

The optimistic teacher is immune to colleagues' jibes. She/he sees good in every pupil. They're all achievers to one degree or another. And Mandy Scoggins is no exception. Whoever she is.

Mandy is oblivious to all this interest in her. In fact she's oblivious to most things at school. She's a survivor, a natural, and she's gonna get there. Wherever "there" is. She's not sure, because she keeps missing geography. Not that she bunks off or anything — she hasn't yet found out which room it gets taught in. That's the trouble when you come from a three-bedroomed flat to a multistorey comprehensive. You can lose your bearings. But it won't be like that in the real world. In the real world the sinks will be over there, the styling chairs over there and the receptionist's desk over there. Because Mandy is going to be a hairdresser. With her own salon. Well, it's an Oxfam shop at the minute, but one day . . . one day!

Mandy and her teacher have a lot in common. They are both optimists. And one day Mandy will do her teacher's hair.

What to look out for:
If you catch your teacher smiling at you out of the corner of their eye, it could be that they're sending you that little message of hope and encouragement that the optimistic teacher often sends. Be careful if you're just about to launch off the high diving board though, because that optimistic teacher could be a closet nasty, who's secretly thinking "Goody! They haven't spotted the piranhas!"

What they teach:
Well, actually, their subject is immaterial, because they teach the little things like "If at first you don't succeed, try, try, try, try, try, try. . ."

What they say:
"I'm sure you could do better."

What they mean:
"Well, I'm not actually sure, but it's worth a try."

Hobbies:
They tend to start things a lot. Finishing is the tricky part. It usually starts with a bang of: "I'm sure I could do that," and ends with a whimper of:
"Er . . . hmmm . . . er." Fishing would suit them, because no-one ever expects a fisherperson to catch anything, or believes them when they do!

How to cope:
Well, blending with the surrounding background is the best form of defence. Looking like everyone who sits near you. This may involve a certain amount of plastic surgery, but it could be worth it!

What excuse will they buy?
Anything that sounds as though you've tried but failed. But at least you tried. The optimist loves a trier. Failure to complete a project due to something mechanical, like a power failure, explosion, air-raid, etc., is acceptable. "I couldn't finish my homework because my pen ran out" does not fall into this category!

Patient Teacher

Nature and habitat:

Teaching requires endless amounts of patience. This is one good reason why I know I could never do it. However, although this is an important feature of the teacher's make-up, few teachers have it. This is of course not so true of the primary school sector, where the accidental mortality rate is much lower. But why should it be that teachers in primary schools require more patience? After all, what they are teaching is far more basic than what is taught in secondary schools, isn't it? I mean to say, do infants do algebra? Logarithms? Animal dissection, apart from during playtime? No. But they do other things that require the patience and understanding of a saint. Like wet themselves. And be sick during school dinners. Mind you, that's more understandable. Their little stomachs haven't built up the necessary resistance to school food that older kids have. They also have more trouble understanding basic concepts — like adding up.

"If I had ten apples, and I ate six, what would I have?"
"Belly ache."

It's surprising, really, that there aren't more bald teachers in primary schools. There are certainly more women teaching in primary schools. Does that mean anything? Are men too clever to teach the little 'uns? Or too frightened? After all, you never know what they're going to throw at you, do you? And a chill goes down the spine as a sweet little squeaky voice says: "Look what I've done, Miss." (Where *is* the school cat, by the way?)

What to look out for:

An indulgent smile, similar to that worn by the kind

teacher. The clothes are similar too (they probably go to the same jumble sales). But, unlike the kind teacher, the patient teacher sighs a lot, just to let you know how patient they are being. Which basically gives the game away. They aren't being patient at all. So watch out, little Johnnie! You're about to lose an arm!

What they teach:
Well, being mainly in primary schools, they teach virtually everything. In secondary schools they teach the sort of subject where it's easy to be patient, because nobody really knows what the subject is!

What they say:
"Oh, Samantha! You're a bit of a one!"

What they mean:
"OK, punk! Make my day!"

Hobbies:
Nothing that requires the slightest patience, obviously. I mean, a normal person only has so much of the stuff, and all their patience has been used up at school. So fishing would be right out. Unless it could be done with a depth charge.

How to cope:
The trick is to know when the patience is going to run out, so that you can make yourself scarce. Foaming at the mouth is usually a bit of a giveaway.

What excuse will they buy?
Your average mixed infant (or even mixed-up infant) would get away with a whiney: "Miiissss . . .", which would immediately be rewarded with an indulgent sigh. But don't try it unless you're unbelievably cute.

Quiet Teacher

Nature and habitat:

Are they there? Are they in the cupboard? Where are they? Aaargh! "Look behind you!" as they say in the best pantomimes. This teacher type can be lethal, especially if you've got a dicky ticker. So, how do they operate? They move quietly around the class, as noiseless as a Ninja. You won't even know they're there. And just as your attention is drifting from your essay to the painter's cradle outside the window . . . (that's very clever! Is he meant to be hanging out by one leg like that, I wonder?) . . . Just as this happens and you're at your most vulnerable . . . pow! He swoops! Or she swoops! Except they don't swoop. Not really. They speak perfectly normally. As normally as any teacher ever speaks. And they say something along the lines of:

"Problems?"

It's probably a genuine offer of help, but the fact that you go "Aaargh!" and leap fourteen feet or the metric equivalent in the air rather gives the game away about your lack of concentration.

This is precisely what the quiet teacher was hoping for. This is why they creep around the classroom. Hoping to catch pupils in the act of minor crimes, like not paying attention. If fate had dealt them a slightly better hand, they could have been a prosecuting barrister (the Latin let them down). Or an undercover agent for MI6 (the striking sticky-out ears gave them away). Or . . . oh! joy of joys! Pinnacle of Pinnacles! A traffic warden! It may not be too late for that, even now, if they give up the badminton and go to Minor Traffic Offences evening classes at the teacher centre. Oh, yes! They may look quiet, but watch out. They

may let you get away with murder in the classroom, but try it on the roads and they'll have you!

What to look out for:
A shiftiness. See if you can catch them peering about when you're not looking. Hang on! That's impossible! Tinted glasses. That's often a sign. You can't quite work out which

way they are looking. Mind you, if they're boss-eyed you won't know whether they're being shifty or not!

What they teach:
The non-practical subjects. Geography, history — anything that involves you spending most of your time sitting at your desk. They do like to know where everyone is at all times. They count you coming into the class, and count you going out again. They'd have you electronically tagged if they could.

What they say:
"Need any help?"

What they mean:
"I know what your game is!"

Hobbies:
Picking little bits of white fluff off black jumpers. Yes, I know it's not really a hobby. Well, not to you and me, that is. But little things amuse little minds, and we're dealing with one of the smallest.

How to cope:
Short of having radar built into your desk there's not a lot you can do.

What excuse will they buy?
Hardly any. Not even the truth. With some teacher-types you just can't win, and this is one of them. Unless of course you casually let drop that one of your parents is the personnel officer responsible for employing traffic wardens.

Riding Teacher....

Nature and habitat:
It's not every school that has a horse. Certainly very few, if any, inner city schools have a horse. In fact some inner city kids think that a horse is something you get in alphabet books, under "H".

We had a horse at our school. For a short time. Until the milkman won it back. After that they banned the playing of poker at our school. At least until the maths teacher could work out an infallible system. So, because of the lack of horses at schools, there is a proportionate lack of riding teachers. But they do exist. They normally teach some other, complementary subject. Like Punjabi or needlecraft. Or astrophysics. But it's in the saddle that they really come alive.

One enterprising school I know doesn't have a horse, but they do have a horseriding club, after school. The club members wear the full gear: jodhpurs, hard hat, rosette with a photo of Captain Mark Phillips in the middle and spurs. They sit astride their chairs and bounce up and down. They get up to quite a gallop, totally destroying the finely polished parquet flooring. The caretaker would have been furious, had he not been a former member of the Chunder and Berkeley Hunt. He still wore a fox tail next to his skin (where exactly I refused to ask, knowing only too well that he would have shown me!). How often he regaled those young Olympic hopefuls with tales of meeting at dawn, downing a few dozen stirrup cups, and then off across the M4 in search of a fox, or a Skoda or anything going slow enough to be caught and ripped to shreds by a pack of beagles!

I feel sorry for the dogs. It's not much of a life really, is

99

it? Not even a dog's life, really. But then it's either hunting with the pack or going up to the research centre to learn how to smoke. Makes you realise that you'd be better off being born a shihtzu doesn't it? (OK, so the name's embarrassing, but at least you get to sit on the furniture and nibble Marks and Spencer's slippers) Or a horse. Nobody messes with horses. Well, circuses stick feathers up their bottoms, but only to make them look pretty. It makes them look silly as well, but that's a by-product. By the same token, nobody messes with horse-riders. You can't reach them for one thing. And they run very fast. And nobody messes with a teacher who spends a lot of time in the saddle.

However, given that most schools don't have a horse, or are ever likely to have a horse, how does a teacher whose field of expertise is horse-riding cope in the school environment? Well, as long as the subject can be likened in some way to the anatomy of a horse, they're fine. So, for instance, the teaching of a language would probably not extend beyond the parts of a horse's body. No "pen of my aunt" nonsense for them! I wonder what the Spanish is for withers? Maths? Well obviously everything would have to be measured in hands. The metric system would leave them totally confused. Football and netball? Everyone would be encouraged to make a clicking noise as they ran around the pitch, to simulate the sound of hooves. And their favourite historical event? You've guessed it! The Charge of the Light Brigade!

What to look for:
Bow-legs. I mean, have you ever seen Clint Eastwood?

What they teach:
Riding, if there's a horse available. Otherwise they fill in. You could find them teaching you almost anything. But they'd give it a horsey bias, as explained above.

What they say:
"You're looking peaky, boy!"

What they mean:
"Needs a damn good rub down with Old Scrotum's Horse Liniment!"

Hobbies:
Well, horse-riding, really. And horse walking, horse sitting, horse standing, horse eating, horse drinking, etc., etc.

How to cope:
Buy a hard hat and a whip.

What excuse will they buy?
Anything involving a horse disease. If you say you were struck down with a bad case of Prickly Horse Blight halfway through your French homework, that should do the trick. However, be careful. You may be expected to swallow an extremely large and unpleasant pill!

Soporific Teacher

Nature and habitat:
It's very embarrassing to fall asleep in class, isn't it? OK, so you don't always get caught out, particularly if your teacher is flash. But what if you were the teacher yourself and everyone was hanging on your every word? Oh, all right, not your every word. Let's face it, there isn't a teacher alive who can expect their class to be interested in everything they say. There aren't many teachers who can honestly say that they expect their class to be interested in *anything* they say. But you never know. So, imagine the embarrassment all round if the class are poised, waiting for a pearl to fall from their mentor's lips, when their mentor falls asleep! Yes! Terrible, eh? But it's quite common. It's a condition known in medical circles as *tiredness*, and many teachers suffer from it.

Put yourself in their shoes, (OK, after you've put in Odour Eaters.) They have to teach the same old stuff day in, day out. You only have to hear it once. In fact, if you're clever, you don't even have to hear it once if you don't want to. Just paint eyeballs on your eyelids and go to sleep. The teacher won't ask you a question. They're too busy trying to stay awake. This system can misfire, of course. I mean to say, you could start to snore for one thing. So check that you don't before you set out on this particular deception. Anyone in your street should be able to tell you whether you snore or not. (Anyone in your town, probably!)

What to look out for:
Closed eyes. That's usually a good sign. Or the fact that the teacher appears to be using the desk to keep upright. In extreme cases they use the desk to get them more comfortable, by lying on it. It's still possible to teach from a prone position, and there's nothing in the NUT handbook to suggest that it's illegal.

What they teach:
Not very much. Given the choice they'd choose a subject that involves the showing of lots of films, since it's much easier to sleep in the dark.

What they say:
"How many times have I told you this?"

What they mean:
"I hope I'm not repeating myself in my sleep."

Hobbies:
Anything restful. Watching TV, videos and bed commercials.

How to cope:
Leave them to it. The risk is that they might forget to tell you something really important. Like the lesson's finished and you can go home!

What excuse will they buy?
"I fell asleep doing my homework." It may work. They should at least be sympathetic.

Tenacious teacher

Nature and habitat:

There are some pupils (come on, admit it!) who treat school like a toilet. By that I mean that they go there regularly but don't get a lot out of it. But these particular pupils actually don't care if they don't get anything out of school. They're not really there to learn. However, when they made this momentous decision about their own education, they hadn't reckoned on the tenacious teacher. For the tenacious teacher will get you educated whether

... and the rivalry between England and Spain which developed into war in the reign of Elizabeth I, while helping to deepen the Protestant sentiments of the English people, was fundamentally economic, brought about by an expanding commercial...

SORRY MUM HE FOLLOWED ME HOME

you want it or not. They'll get those facts into your brain by any route possible. Up your nose if necessary. Because they are *tenacious*. They'll even teach you what it means. But until they do, you'll have to make do with the dictionary definition, which gives us:

Tenacious: Adj. 1. holding firmly 2. strongly cohesive or adhesive 3. persistent.

The tenacious teacher is all these things. Certainly sticky! They'll badger and bulldoze until, weak with resisting, you give in and learn things. The fact that you instantly forget things again doesn't bother the tenacious one. Their task is achieved. They move on to the next great learning hurdle. They are like Hannibal (although some of them look more like his elephants), scaling mountains of ignorance.

But why do they do it? Well, it's possible that they didn't work very hard at school, and they now regret it. So they're taking it out on you. That's not fair! It's not your fault! You weren't even there when they were daydreaming out of the window, were you? Anyway, it never did them any harm. I mean to say, they did a minimum of work and they wound up teaching. Ah! Just a minute. Maybe that's the punishment!

What to look out for:
There's a sort of intense look in the eyes. A look that says "I'm here to improve your mind!" But don't stare back. It can work like hypnosis.

What they teach:
Anything and everything! They don't mind. They'll give up their free periods to take spare classes. They've even been known to poison the tea of the less eager colleagues, in order to get greater access to young minds.

What they say:
"Let me just go over that again."

What they mean:
"I'm going to teach you this if I have to knock it into your head with a sledgehammer!"

Hobbies:
There's no time for hobbies! Unless it's taking children for private tuition. They might join the scouts, as long as they're allowed to do all the teaching of knots and stuff.

How to cope:
This is a tricky one. It's a bit like trying to tell you how to cope with unwanted door-to-door evangelists. The answer is don't open the door in the first place. But it isn't until you open the door that you realise what you've let yourself in for. And the same is roughly true of this type of teacher. Only worse. You could go to school with a sound- and light-proof sack over your head, but the tenacious one would still get in somehow!

What excuse will they buy?
They won't take no for an answer. On the other hand, they're so busy pumping you full of new facts, they probably won't notice that you haven't done your home-work on the last lot yet!

Useless Teacher —

Nature and habitat:
In just the same way that most schools have a couple of really good teachers, they also have a few bad ones. It's not their fault. They're bright and personable, but just not any good. It's sad really. They try quite hard. It just doesn't happen.

I had one at my old school. In fact, she pinched my desk for three weeks until someone pointed out to her that she was supposed to be standing at the front of the class, teaching it. But she got there in the end. And it only took

five years. Her problem was that, like so many other teachers, she'd gone from school to college and back to school again, and she found it hard to make the adjustment from sitting in a desk to standing in front of one.

Of course there are some teachers who think that the only difference between a teacher and a pupil is the direction they face in the class. The pupils face the front wall and the teacher faces the back wall. I thought I'd clear that up in case anyone was in any doubt. It's not always the case, of course. There are kids who spend more time facing backwards, chatting to the kid behind. I knew a kid in my class who always faced backwards. He sat in the back row, talking to the wall. But they moved him to a special unit, where he was much happier. The walls were much closer, and padded, which made them look a lot friendlier. He's done very well for himself. He's gone into politics. Joined the Green Party. Well, it was either that or become a teacher.

But the thing about useless teachers is that you learn so much from them. Well, not actually from them because they don't know anything. Not even the time of day. Well, that's not strictly true. They know that the big hand's on the something and the little hand isn't. But the way you learn from them is by *teaching* them. And teaching is a learning experience. What sort of things do you learn? Where the pencils are kept (in the cupboard with the cowardly teacher). The difference between a pencil and a biro. The stuff that will stand you in great stead in the Real World. Because the Real World is tough and hard, and the person who doesn't know where the pencils are kept hasn't got a chance. For in six days did God make Heaven and Earth, and on the seventh day He looked for somewhere to keep the pencils.

What to look out for:
Anyone who looks totally confused, but isn't in short

trousers with a runny nose. Or even a short nose and runny trousers. That's probably a kid from the nearby primary school with a note for the French teacher (He'll marry her, you mark my words!). No, the useless teacher looks more or less adult and totally confused. But don't approach them unless you want to spend the rest of your school days answering silly questions.

What they teach:
It's hard to tell. I doubt if even they can tell you.

What they say:
"Put your hands up, class!"
What they mean:
"Right. So that's the class then, is it?"

Hobbies:
Painting by numbers. Sculpting by numbers. Shopping by numbers. Sitting perfectly still by numbers. Anything by numbers, really. Which is a pity because they're useless at maths!

How to cope:
There are a couple of ways around the situation of being confronted by the useless teacher. You can sit very quietly and let them work things out for themselves, in which case they will quite probably self-destruct. Or you can help them. Answer questions and generally improve their mind. But be careful if you take this course of action. They could develop into an intelligent teacher or much much worse!

What excuse will they buy?
Anything, as long as it's said slowly and repeated until they've grasped the concept. "I forgot my book" is a little too complicated. "I went shopping instead" would be easier to understand. But make sure that you've got their full attention first, or the explanation could take days.

Varsity Teacher

Nature and habitat:

What's he on about? I can hear some of you saying. What's "varsity" when it's at home? Cor! He's really scraping the barrel now! Why didn't he pick "vicious teacher"? There's plenty of those about. Or "ventriloquist teacher". That's the type that makes little noises and blames it on you. They're only doing it to pick a fight. They're just another branch of the nasty teacher family, really. So, what is the varsity teacher? Well, varsity, as I'm sure you all know really, is the trendy way that some people refer to university. Usually people who've been there. So a varsity teacher is one that has been to university. But they've *all* been to university, haven't they? Not all of them, no. But even if they have, very few teachers make a thing of it.

They went, they learned, they left. End of story. But not so the varsity teacher. He/she wishes they were still there, instead of teaching scruffy kids in Gusset Street Comprehensive. Their teaching consists more of debate than teaching:

"OK. Let's discuss the arms race."
(*Hand up.*)
"Is that anything like the three-legged race, sir?"
(*Great sighs from varsity teacher.*)

They have failed to realise that the pupils in their charge are (a) at least ten years younger than they are, and (b) at least ten *light* years less educated than they are.

"Right. Get your books out!"

And while the class stare vacantly at their books, Varsity stares longingly out of the window, drifting back to the dreaming spires of Oxford. Punting on the river. Cream teas. The boat race. Food fights in local restaurants. Making total Rodneys of themselves while they were still young enough to get away with it. Ah! Happy days!

He gets jolted back to reality.

"Sorry to interrupt you, sir. But Hodges has just been sick!"

What to look out for:
The scarf. They still wear the university scarf, all year round. It's probably not even the original. They keep having to get it replaced as it falls apart. On weekends they probably wear a Tee-shirt that reads: *I Went To Oxford And All I Got Was This Lousy Masters Degree In Psychology With Honours*.

What they teach:
I know exactly what they would *like* to teach. They would like to teach *somewhere else*!

113

What they say:
"In a perfect world . . ."

What they mean:
"When I was at Oxford . . ."

Hobbies:
Trips to Oxford. Failing that, watching videos of films that take place in Oxford. Their favourite TV programme is *Inspector Morse*. But the plot is impossible for anyone else in the room to follow, because Varsity keeps calling out:

"I've been there!"
"I walked down that lane!"
"I've been mugged in that shopping precinct!"
"I've thrown up over that dog!"

Not that the plots are easy to follow anyway. Not without a university degree!

How to cope:
Support Oxford United? Wear blue? I don't know! Frankly, I don't think there's anyway of ingratiating yourself with this teacher type. Obviously you could go to university and then return to your old school on a visit. But by then you'll probably find that they've grown up into a completely different type, and don't want to know you! Whatever you do, don't feel inadequate. If you're less intelligent than the varsity teacher, it's up to them to do something about it! Like leave!

What excuse will they buy?
Well, naturally it has to be long and complex, and preferably total Gobbledee-Gook. The best thing to do is to memorise a few pages of a computer magazine and hit them with that. They'll be totally impressed, not to say confused. It'll take you several days to do it, though, so you might be better off doing your homework in the first place!

Worried teacher....

Nature and habitat:

Don't mistake this for the harassed type. Mind you, you couldn't really because this type doesn't move with anything like the speed of the harassed. In fact, this one rarely moves at all. They just stand there looking worried. Naturally you imagine that there's something wrong. But if you ask, they just say: "No, no!" breezily. Which naturally makes you feel that you've done something. Like got the answer wrong. Or got the answer right. Who knows? You certainly don't! I mean, if you were that sure of the answer you wouldn't need to be taught it, would you?

The problem is that whatever is worrying the worried teacher probably has nothing whatever to do with you. Or even to do with school. It could be something like: "Did I lock the back door when I came out this morning?" Not that your average teacher has got anything worth pinching. Unless you count those Greek bookends bought on last year's school trip from an old street trader with an incurable skin condition. Even now the teacher won't pick them up to dust them without wearing rubber gloves. Mind you, the worried teacher tends to wear rubber gloves for everything. They'd wear them to teach in, if it weren't for the fact that it could be insulting to the pupils. Still, it's another thing to worry about, isn't it?

And that's what they do best — worry. They worry about everything. If the exam results are bad, they worry that they're not teaching well enough. If the exam results are good, they worry in case they're teaching too well. As we've discovered earlier, one teacher teaching harder than the others could upset the overall balance. Or make the pupils realise that there's more to school than keeping the teacher locked in the cupboard or continually telling it where the pencils are kept.

If the worried teacher has to have the day off (usually due to worry), they worry about whether their class is being taught properly. After all, it was very last-minute, and the only supply teacher available was Mrs Millet, who spent her entire full-time teaching career with the army. At best she'll keep the class amused with tales about her travels. At worst she might teach them to strip a Bren gun. Very worrying! Still, the marching and sit-ups won't do them any harm. Hopefully!

So why do they teach if they worry so much? Well, it might be because they were told that they'd make good teachers because they were caring and patient. Very useful qualities for a teacher. Almost as useful as a ready wit and martial arts training. They probably then worried that if they didn't become a teacher, they'd regret the decision. So here they are. Worrying. The irony is that if they stopped worrying, they'd probably be no good!

What to look for:
Bitten nails (if you can bear to get that close). In extreme cases, nervous perspiration. Yuck!

What they teach:
Unfortunately for them (and indirectly for you) they never teach the straightforward subjects like history that deal in facts, dates, and incontrovertible data. They teach subjects that are open to interpretation, where opinions rather than facts matter. That's the problem. They're too worried to have an opinion in case they're wrong.

What they say:
"Yes . . ."

What they mean:
"Oh, dear . . ."

Hobbies:
Hobbies are a problem, really. What if the phone goes or the cat wants to come in? Putting the TV on is also a bit tricky. What if the aerial gets struck by lightning? It can happen, even in the middle of summer. They quite like watching the news and weather, although it's always a bit worrying. There was some chap in America who went completely mental in a shopping mall with a machine gun. And, yes, OK, it was three thousand miles away and the police shot him dead, but you never know . . . he could get better and come over here. Better avoid the corner shop for a few months.

How to cope:
You could try telling the teacher not to worry. But then they'll only worry that their worrying has reached such a pitch that even a schoolchild can recognise it! I suppose you could slip something into their tea. I think Bob Martins do a mind tranquilliser.

What excuse will they buy?
It depends whether you want to worry them or not. It would be better for them if you just said: "I haven't done my project work because I couldn't be bothered!" That would give them the opportunity to be angry for a change. Although, knowing your luck, it will simply make them worry that they're setting you too much work! You simply can't win with this one!

EXTREME CASE OF BITTEN NAILS

X-Ray of teachers

Throughout this book I've been putting teachers under the microscope. Now I've managed to get one on the X-ray table. I think this one is fairly typical.

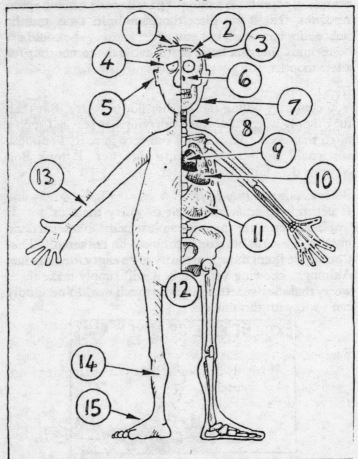

1 *Top of the head*: this is where teachers get most of their ideas from.

2 *Brain*: small. Hurts very easily.

3 *Mind*: orderly. Neat little compartments that are very interchangeable, so that they can change their mind as often as possible.

4 *Eyes*: highly developed to spot mischief at a hundred metres. Swivel-action allows them to turn a blind eye to anything that looks like it might mean them getting involved.

5 *Inner and outer ear*: developed in much the same way as the eyes. Also fitted with the optional swivel, for cocking a deaf ear.

6 *Nasal cavity*: can detect bodily gases, and even pinpoint whose body they came out of! Also fitted with a swivel at the end, so that it can be turned up at homework handed in late.

7 *Jaw*: very flexible. Can go from a wide-open shout position to a twisted sneer in a hundredth of a second.

8 *Neck*: also flexible. Useful for craning into corners and detecting trouble.

9 *Heart*: varies greatly in size from teacher to teacher. Can be as large as the whole teacher or practically non-existent.

10 *Lungs*: highly developed over years of classroom control.

11 *Stomach*: strong. Developed over years of dinner duties and watching school plays.

12 *Naughty bits*: teachers don't have them, do they?

13 *Arm muscles*: going to waste from neglect, due to banning of the cane.

14 *Leg muscles*: highly developed over years of moving from classroom to classroom.

15 *Feet*: very smelly.

Y-bother Teacher...

Nature and habitat:

You've probably heard this a million times: "I don't know why I bother!" Many different types of teacher say this. Probably most of them. But there is a particular type who make it their clarion call. They throw up their hands in despair every five minutes, just because you don't grasp the full meaning of something first go. That's not fair, is it? A lot of this stuff is tricky. They know the ins and outs. They've read the book. You haven't even *seen* the book. Well, you have. It's in your desk, actually, but how are you supposed to know that unless the teacher tells you? For heaven's sake, that's why they say stuff like: "Get out your books," isn't it? After all, if they're not asking you to get out your book because the thing they want to teach you is *in* the book, what are they asking you to get out your book for?

"Get out your books. We're going to have a bonfire!"
"Get out your books. A storm of killer locusts is about to attack the school, and you'll need to defend yourselves!"
"Get out your books. The rag and bone man is in the street outside!"

No, none of these scenarios seem likely. So the book getting-out must be directly linked to the passing on of knowledge. Once you've worked that out you can proceed. But how is the poor brain going to cope with such a complex concept if it doesn't get a gently nudge from the teacher? In days gone by, of course, the brain got a gentle nudge from the book itself, thus cutting out the middle man. The teacher was only really there to make sure book and brain connected. This usually involved a sharp, swift

arm-movement, bringing book and brain into close contact, and forcing the knowledge through the skull. Of course, with the march of progress teaching methods have changed. They've become more subtle. I don't think they even teach the sharp arm movement any more at teacher training camp. I checked this with a typical Y-bother teacher, and this was what I heard.

"Yeah. You're right. It isn't. It's just part and parcel of the so-called March of Progress. Are you writing this down? Good. *And don't ask me how to spell it, for goodness sake*! In my young days you knew where you were. Teaching methods were more straightforward. Facts were imparted, kids absorbed them, you checked they'd been listening, and on to the next fact. Anyone who couldn't keep up was made to stand in the corner in a bucket of quick-drying cement. That usually sorted them out. If it didn't there was always the threat of death by vaulting horse, parallel bars or sports master's jockstrap. For anyone who was being really slow (i.e. unable to work out a logarithm without looking it up) there was always the ultimate: melted *Good Boy Choccy Drops* smeared on the buttocks, then locked in the chalk cupboard with Mr Girder's Irish Wolfhound. Now it's all reasonableness and patience. You're not even allowed to beat up the parents. I don't know why I bother!"

I had to stop there, because the teacher started to foam at the mouth. And I'd thought she looked such a nice little old lady, too!

What to look out for:
Difficult. Appearances can be deceptive, because this is an attitude of mind, really. It wouldn't even be fair to say that this type tend to be older, because some young teachers give up pretty early on (although this can be due to frustration over the shortage of pretty coloured chalk).

What they teach:
Again it's usually the basics. The ones you really need to give you a good start in life. I mean, you can always catch up on stuff like Mandarin Chinese once you've made it to Governor of the Bank of England. (Actually, that's not much of a job — putting your autograph on banknotes all day. Might just as well be a popstar!)

What they say:
"Good morning, class!"

What they mean:
"I don't know why I bother!"

Hobbies:
They live in the past, irrespective of how old they are. They hunger for Victorian values, the return of the birch, and suspender belts. They can remember when a ten pence bag of crisps was fourpence, and Britannia ruled the waves. They love watching old films: weepies or war, they don't mind which. Often they're the same thing. And they're great collectors: stamps, train numbers, labels off bottles, dead animals, anything.

How to cope:
Work hard and smile. It's your only chance. But even still they'll turn their nose up at you and say: "I don't know why I bother!" I don't know why *you* bother, really!

What excuse will they buy?
Don't waste your powers of invention coming up with anything clever, subtle or so far-fetched that it just *has* to be true. They won't even ask if you've brought your kit, done your homework, dissected the frog, or whatever it is you're endeavouring to get out of. They'll assume you haven't done any work, even if you have, just so that they can say: "I don't know why I bother!"

Z-teacher (headteacher)

Nature and habitat:
The ultimate prize in some teachers' minds. The ultimate insult in others. There are two main ways someone becomes headteacher:

1 By showing instinctive management skills and becoming the obvious choice for such an exalted position;
2 By mistake.

There are other ways of course: being promoted beyond your level of incompetence, walking past the door as the previous head shoots himself, coming to clean the window at a school that's short-staffed, etc. But these are not the usual ways.

So what is a headteacher? Speaking from personal experience of my own childhood, it's someone who fills in for teachers who are ill and sets back the entire form's development by about three years. My headmaster was a wonderful old boy. The teachers really liked him, especially when he forgot to turn up. Sometimes he would turn up, but think he was still at home. He got quite cross one day when he thought one of us had tarmacked his back garden. Still, he had the fifth year out in the playground with road drills digging it up to make room for a rosebed. (That was a useful learning experience for the fifth year, as it turned out, because most of them took up road working as a career. It's not a bad job for anyone who likes travelling — very slowly.)

There are of course perks to being a headteacher. You get to go home early, and the local authority provide free riot gear. Oh, and you get your own little room with a choice of decor: painted, papered or padded.

What to look out for:
The headteacher is a barometer for the rest of the staff. That is to say, when they're harassed he's relaxed, and vice-versa. But the head is always easy to spot. They're always in their office. Oh, yes — if you're lucky you might see them in assembly, for the schools that still have them, otherwise you can go through your entire school career, and at the end of it wonder who the heck the person shaking your hand is.

What they teach:
For those that venture out of their office — anything they can get their hands on. The cowardly teacher usually makes a good headteacher, although they have to have their office made smaller.

What they say:
"Hello, I'm the headteacher."

What they mean:
"I really ought to get out more."

125

Hobbies:

They used to have a lot of time on their hands. But now that many schools have to handle their own finances, headteachers spend all their free time at evening classes learning "business studies". That's adult language for adding up. You'd think they'd just nip into the back of a maths class, wouldn't you? Except, of course, they know that they'd come out more confused than they were when they went in. They know just how useless the maths teacher is – after all, they appointed him!

How to cope:

There's really not much need to worry, since you may never meet your headteacher. It's best to be prepared, though. If approached by the headteacher, the best form of defence is to get in first, before they speak. Say something like: "Excuse me! Could you tell me the way to the science block, please?"

This will throw them completely on a number of counts, including:

a) they'll assume that you're from another school. Don't worry about being in uniform. They won't recognise it. It's more than likely been modernised since they last ventured out of their office.

b) they'll be disturbed that they can't remember where the science block is, having totally forgotten that it was blown up only last week (they missed the funeral due to leaving their diary in their gardening jacket at school).

Either way, they will scuttle back into their office, vowing never to leave it ever again!

What excuse will they buy?

Well, to be honest, you are never really going to find yourself in the situation of needing to make excuses to the Head Teacher. After all, the chances are they won't even realise that you are a pupil at their school, even if you're in full uniform!

Well these are the teacher types I managed to track down. I feel sure that there are many more, but these were more than enough for me!

On my travels around the schools I made some random jottings (on walls, desks, bald heads, etc.). I have collated them into some sort of order, and turned them into an appendix. Yes! I've still got my appendix! and here it is!

Appendix 1: How Can You Tell if Your teacher is an Alien?

It's quite possible that other galaxies have infiltrated our schools by sending aliens from their planets. But how can you tell? Obviously an extra arm, several heads or a completely purple body would give you a bit of a clue, but it wouldn't be proof positive. Anyway, aliens aren't that stupid. I mean you don't spend thousands of light years developing the space technology and fighting off the Green Lobby (although in outer space it's probably the Yellow Lobby or something) who keep saying that more money should be spent on protecting the planet, not wasted on space travel, only to arrive on Earth disguised as a teacher and have some spotty kid come up to you and say: "Oi! You're an alien, ain't yer?"

No! Aliens are not that stupid! In fact, they have been coming to Earth for years, cunningly disguised as more or less human beings, to corrupt the minds of our youth. It may seem strange, but it's not impossible. They've already infiltrated television. You may have noticed how large numbers of seemingly talentless people are suddenly cropping up on every other programme, displaying no particular skill but winning the hearts of the viewers with their strange *magnetism*. Of course in the early days their technology was far from perfect, and the aliens didn't quite get the proportions right. They either made their "humans" too large (Patrick Moore) or too small (Ronnie Corbett). Recent models have been almost undetectable from the real thing, with a few exceptions (Russell Grant, Wincey Willis).

However, having conquered the media they decided to move into schools. After all, our children are our future, it says in some song or another. And they also have pocket money to spend, which is what it's all about. Big business. You see, other galaxies have done away with junk food. They've realised that it's bad for you, harms the environment, and generates so much methane that everyone's afraid to strike a match. So what can these other galaxies do with their surplus stocks? Flog them to earth, that's what. And that's where the alien teachers come in. They teach unsuspecting schoolchildren that there's more nutritional value in a NergaWoggaSlurfburger from the ninth galaxy, and the kids rush home and badger their mum to go and buy some. Just then a travelling burger salesman (alien, of course) arrives on the front doorstep of Tesco's head office, and off-loads the lot. Brilliant!

So, how can you detect that your teacher is an alien? Asking a simple question that every Earth person would know the answer to would be the quickest way. But there are a couple of stumbling blocks in this otherwise totally foolproof and perfect plan:

1) How do we find a question that we can be absolutely certain every Earth dweller knows the answer to?
2) Even if we find the question, how can we be certain that, just because the "teacher" failed to answer the question, they are actually an alien? They might be just a particularly bad, stupid teacher.

All of which rather suggests that there is no foolproof way of discovering whether or not your teacher is an alien. I mean to say, it's no good relying on irrational behaviour, sudden foaming at the mouth or any of the signs that might suggest that a human being wasn't all they were cracked up to be. These sorts of things are normal behaviour for teachers. Oh, yes, I suppose if you really think you have grounds for suspecting your teacher is an alien, you could take their shoes off to see if they've got webbed feet, or cut them in half to count their lungs or see if their blood is orange with little mauve flecks, but you're going to feel a bit silly if your suspicions turn out to be groundless, aren't you? How embarrassing! No! I think the only answer is to leave it to the experts, and watch out for anything unrecognisable appearing on the school dinner-plates. Although even that will be nothing unusual!

Appendix 2:
Where do teachers go on Holiday?

This is a question on everybody's lips. Partly because they want to know which places to avoid, and partly because they're envious of those lovely long holidays! And who wouldn't be? Boy, oh boy! Of course most teachers will try to make out they're so exhausted by the end of term that they spent the entire summer in hospital, which would explain the shortage of beds. But that's just them whingeing, trying to get sympathy. They've got to be joking, haven't they? After all that extra homework they gave you last term, the last thing they deserve is your sympathy!

But where do they go? Well, I was able to swap postcards, slides and little plaster souvenirs with the staff of a school near me, and this is what I found out:

Eastbourne: where Mr Guffter, head of English, did in fact get a chance to have a rest, once he had put everyone under forty in detention.

Skegness: this is for the slightly more adventurous teacher, who fancies a good old fashioned English holiday. And Mrs Pencil (metalwork and hang-gliding) had a wonderful time. Unfortunately nobody else in Skegness did, because she spent the entire holiday on the beach making all the little kids hold their spades properly. She then embarrassed her family by telling Mr Punch that he ought to be ashamed of himself.

Greece: this is for the historically minded teacher, like Mrs Massive. Unfortunately she could not abide the fact that the Greek tourist guide spoke English so badly:

"Earizcropplesinnit."
"No, no, young man! Listen (*pronouncing perfectly*): 'There is the Acropolis'."

132

"Nah! Thereiz Multi-Stori-Car-park. Earizcropplesinnit."
"I don't know why I bother!"

Still, she got a nice suntan and an offer of marriage. At least, I think it was marriage. The language barrier got in the way!

Rome: where Miss Timbling, biology (and also in charge of chalk distribution), visited the Vatican and did a bit of brass rubbing. All went well until some chap in a red frock stood in her light. Still, she soon sent him packing with a flea in his ear. "I don't care if he is the Pope!" she told alarmed bystanders.

France: and an opportunity for Mr Gerbil, head of languages, to hear French spoken properly, not crucified as it is by the inmates of Sir Oswald Bypass County Secondary School. In fact, not only an opportunity to hear it spoken but also a chance to have a shot at doing it himself. He proudly ordered a bottle of the local wine but unfortunately, due to a quirk of the local dialect, got an operation for piles instead. Still it was quick, and he was able to drive afterwards.

Spain: where it was fiesta time. Mrs Semtex, Head of Lower School, was able to witness at first hand the spectacle of the bull-run, where a bull runs free in the streets and the young bloods of the town attempt to catch it. The poor bull caught sight of her on the hotel balcony, turned tail and was never seen again! The townsfolk were furious. They had to live on pilchard sandwiches for the next three months.

The Mediterranean: should have been the perfect setting for a relaxing holiday for Mrs Playtex, the games mistress, and Eric Wirzel, history and religious studies. But they came home after two days, having bumped into every child in her class!

Butlins: Mr Euphony and Miss Phooey, the twin terrors of the Upper Fifth (liberal studies and astrophysics respectively) did what they do every year. Separate rooms at a Butlin Theme Hotel. "Not as nice as the camps, and the lamb cutlets have been cold three years running." However, they had a wonderful time playing Hunt the Custard, and Miss Phooey won thirty-seven pee at bingo so they'll definitely go back next year.

THERE'S MELVIN PARSLEY FROM 4B.. AND HE'S SMOKING

Of the rest of the staff, most stayed at home, two went rambling in the Costwolds, one went to a Friends of the Earth protest march, and one went into the stocks for non-payment of poll tax.

The general feeling among the staff who went abroad (those who are not still in quarantine) was that going abroad was all right, but there are far too many foreigners there.

Appendix 3:
.. If I was not a teacher...

I'm not referring to me personally, you understand. I'm not a teacher. No way! Never, ever! Phew! You're joking, squire! Anyway, I'm not. But I know a large number. At least I do now after researching this book. And one thing I've discovered is that many teachers believe that they are not trained for any other job. And yet 6000 teachers left the profession in 1989 alone. So, where did they go? What jobs do teachers do if they leave teaching? Well, I have assessed the suitability of various jobs, and here are my findings:

Dustman: lets start with the sort of job a teacher might be qualified to do. Early start in the morning. That wouldn't bother a teacher — they're used to getting up early. Whether they're used to *waking* up early is a different matter! It's a dirty job, but then so is teaching. You only have to look at the state of some of our schools to realise that. Tips at Christmas. That would be a bonus! Usually nobody even thanks a teacher. But I'm not sure that a teacher would be emotionally suited to a job as a dustman (or refuse disposal operative), because they'd be forever telling people off for not packing their rubbish neatly in the bin. They'd make them do it again and again until they got

GOOD WORK MR SAUNDERS, YOUR BIN LINER IS MUCH BETTER PACKED TODAY it right. Then, and only then, would they take the bin away. Then, and only then, would they spill most of it on the path!

Barrister: again a job where a good all-round education might come in handy. And it probably wouldn't bother them having to study law. It would make a pleasant change going back to school and being taught. But again they're not suited. They'd be forever shouting at the judge: "Don't interrupt while I'm talking! See me afterwards."

Accountant: Yes, possibly the sort of job for a maths teacher, except that accounting is a creative art (at least it can be) whereas maths is an exact science. Plus the fact that when you're doing someone's accounts the answers aren't in the back of the book!

Chef: could suit a home economics teacher. After all, it's only cooking. But there's one big difference. The food cooked in restaurants is cooked for paying customers. Customers who expect to like the meal. Customers who expect the meal to like them and stay in their stomachs for more than ten minutes, or at least until they get outside. Whereas the food cooked in school by pupils is not expected to be fit for human consumption. It's intended as a learning experience. And the surviving relatives of the child doing the cooking usually learn never to let that child anywhere near the cooker again!

I think this example throws up (unfortunate choice of words, I know) the big difference between teachers and everyone else. Teachers live in an institutionalised world where things are theoretical rather than practical, and have little or nothing to do with the real world. Let out, they simply wouldn't cope with Real Life. I think it would be better and safer for everyone concerned if they all remained in an institution!

Appendix 4:
The Secrets of the Staffroom!

What goes on behind that impenetrable door? Well, disguising myself cunningly as a small boy with a note (in which disguise I had four offers of marriage from various members of staff, I might add!) I infiltrated the staffroom. Naturally I was kept waiting for many hours as the teachers played, "Well, I'm not going to ask who it's for. I might have to get involved". But I was in no hurry to reveal my note, since it was in fact a completely blank piece of paper. This was an oversight, and the only flaw in an otherwise perfect plan. It was also, incidentally, a fact that went entirely unnoticed by the teacher who eventually read the blank note. "Right," they said. "I'll get one of the bigger boys on to it right away," and screwed the blank paper up and threw it at the mounting pile of screwed-up bits of paper beside the wastepaper basket. Gosh! Does this room *never* get cleaned? Apparently not. I was told that the contract cleaners, Squeekikleen Limited, flatly refused to go near the place since Mrs Tasker gave them a few sharp words about the spelling of their name. It was either that that frightened them off, or Mr Gerbil asking them for help with his *Sun* crossword!

But what an Aladdin's cave that place is! The things I saw! The things I heard! The stories I could tell! If I sold my story to the *News of the World*, I'd have more money than I could spend in a lifetime! Unfortunately they refused to let me out of the staffroom unless I agreed to keep quiet about what I'd seen. They threatened me: lines, detention, double French, everything! What could I do! Call me a wimp, but you would have done the same! As for the secrets of the staffroom . . . they must remain secret, I'm afraid!

Appendix 5: I Play Dirty!

Assuming that the teacher who had directed me to ENSA instead of MENSA had done it on purpose, and was being devious rather than stupid, I thought I also should have a go at playing dirty, even though it is against my nature. I mean, the naughtiest thing I've ever done is lift the toilet seat in a convent. However, I decided that the end justified the means, and restored to playing dirty.

BUGS! Yes! I used bugs! By which I don't mean that I stuck a plastic cockroach in a teacher's desk. No! I am talking surveillance equipment. Now you'd be amazed just how easy it is to lay your hands on this sort of stuff. It was an education, I can tell you. And, naturally, the more you pay, the more sophisticated it becomes. Starting at around five pounds for an inter-connecting room listening device, which turned out to be a glass that you held against the wall, the range covered absolutely everything. The most amazing thing I was offered included a bug "no larger than an ant's nostril", that could pick up the sound of someone scratching their bottom at a hundred yards! Unfortunately, it also picked up anyone else scratching their bottom in the intermediate area. So what you actually heard was something that sounded exactly like someone with a flat-top sandpapering their head. However, it was during my journey into the murky world of phone-tapping and room-bugging, that I met up again with Elderado Dingbatti.

~~Love Miranda Bootle~~

Appendix 6: Elderado Dingbatti – The man and the Legend:

Those of you who have read *Coping with Parents* will know only too well that Elderado was one of my team of experts. For those of you who have not read *Coping With Parents*, I should perhaps tell you that Elderado was one of my team of experts. There. Now we all know who he is. I will also mention at this point that his contribution to that book could be summed up in two words. But instead I'll just say that he contributed nothing. In fact I had hoped never to see him again. Indeed, I had not expected to see him again, certainly not so soon. I had no idea he was out. He explained, over a mug of hot Coca-cola in a back street mission, that he had been moved from the High Security Holiday Camp for the Criminally Insane to a "half-way" hostel, recently set up in a disused "Toys-Я-Us." He was making great progress, he told me. His social worker was very pleased with him. He hadn't killed anyone for, oh, days.

"How can I help you, Melvin?" he asked. He never did get the hang of my name. To be honest, I wasn't sure that he could. And I was about to tell him so, when I heard a mouth which turned out to be mine say: "Surveillance equipment". Well, this turned out to be a magic phrase. Surveillance equipment was obviously something that excited Eldorado greatly. That much was clear immediately. What was less obvious immediately was the fact that he knew absolutely nothing about it.

However, we arranged to meet later that night, up a tree. Yes. That's right. I did write "up" a tree. Not "by" a tree, or "near" a tree. "Less conspicuous," Elderado said. No-one would suspect us of being engaged in anything underhand. No! He was right there! Any passer-by would simply think we were mad, and in his case they'd be right! How on earth did they let him out? What story did he tell them to convince them that he should be allowed to move unhindered among an unsuspecting public? Choosing my words carefully (after all, even if he did think *I* was a decent sort of bloke, *he* was a homicidal maniac), I asked him. His reply, if I heard him correctly, astounded me. I say "if I heard him correctly" because a passing squirrel chose that precise moment to stuff his nuts in my ear. But I believe that he said that the reason he was released was because he had expressed a deep desire to become a TEACHER! Yes! He did! A TEACHER! And WHAT IS MORE, THEY LET HIM OUT! I know there's a teacher shortage, but that's taking things a little far, isn't it? To say that I was flabbergasted is an understatement. I nearly fell out of the tree. If it hadn't been for the courting couple on the bench below I would have done. Where was he hoping to teach? I asked him.

"In a private school," he replied. Ah. Perhaps he wasn't so mad after all!

If you like to laugh, you'll be howling for hours with HIPPO's hilarious selection of joke books . . .

Kids' Best Jokes   *Compiled by Karen King*
Long jokes, short jokes, fat jokes, thin jokes . . . they're all shapes and sizes in *Kids' Best Jokes*. But something all these jokes do have in common is that each one is somebody's favourite!   £1.75

The School Joke Book   *Susannah Bradley*
Here's a joke book with a difference. It's huge and it's full of pictures! There's a joke for every school occasion – in the classroom, in the cloakroom, in the toilets, behind the bike sheds . . . – and they're all told by a bunch of crazy cartoon kids! Even the most boring teacher will roar with laughter! £2.50

The Cops 'n' Robbers Joke Book
                               Laura Norder
Did you ever read a joke with a police siren on the top? Well, now's your chance . . .
   Follow the antics of Burglar Bill, Smasher Smith and Sneaky Sid as they try to escape the clutches of Detective Golightly, P.C. Pouncer and W.P.C. Perfect (not forgetting Woofer the police dog).   £1.75

Father Christmas' Joke Book   *Terry Deary*
At last, Father Christmas has put pen to paper and, with the help of his seven gnomes, he tells you just what Christmas is *really* like at the North Pole (whilst the gnomes tell you just what Father Christmas is *really* like!). Then there are gnome jokes, gnock, gnock jokes, cracker jokes and lots lots more, to make sure this Christmas is truly crazy!   £1.75